TAILWIND

TAILWIND

The Robert E. Miller Story

To Sharon and Tony
With Love.

Bob

7/20/19

JENNIFER TYLER

NICHOLAS YOUNES

Tailwind: The Robert E. Miller Story
By Jennifer Tyler and Nicholas Younes

Copyright © 2019 by The E. Stanley Jones Foundation

Published by
The E. Stanley Jones Foundation
Email: info@estanleyjonesfoundation.com
www.estanleyjonesfoundation.com

Cover and Interior Design: Shivraj K. Mahendra
www.shivrajmahendra.com

ISBN: 978-1092213172

MANUFACTURED IN THE USA

CONTENTS

PREFACE

by Jennifer Tyler

Most people quietly live life without ever considering a book may one day be written about them. For some, modesty precludes thought that such a book would hold any interest to the outside world.

What about you? Seriously? What would you consider book-worthy about your life and do you think it would be of interest to others? Answering these questions will give you some insight as to why Robert Eugene Miller resisted the idea.

I have known Bob and Nadine Miller for many years. I first met them at a United Christian Ashram meeting in

Ruston, Louisiana. My company, Tyler Associates, had been retained by the United Christian Ashram to conceptualize and communicate a vision, and to design and implement a feasibility study to assess constituent feedback, aimed toward sustaining the Ashram ministry. Having completed my work, I was in Ruston to give a report to the board. Robert Eugene Miller was on that board.

The Millers were out of the country when I was in personal conversations with other board members and key donors as a part of the study, but they managed to be in town for this important meeting.

Dinner followed the report and discussion, and it was my good fortune to sit near Bob and Nadine Miller. Aware of their admiration for E. Stanley Jones, architect of the Christian Ashram in the United States, I was eager to hear their thoughts. I found myself an observer of enjoyable exchanges between Bob, Nadine, and their friends. I suppose this evening laid the foundation for our long, trusted friendship. The dynamic between the Millers was infectious. All I knew about Bob before that evening was his reputation as an entrepreneur who had made his mark in the oil and gas industry and as a philanthropist. There was so much more to discover.

Later, Bob told me about the Mission he had established, which served the needs of homeless people. As admirable as that was, I would soon learn that the Mission was only the tip of a large iceberg of other worth-while causes that interested Bob Miller.

With Bob Miller, if you want to get to his back-story, you must pass through his considerable reserve and sincere humility. If you asked me to describe Bob Miller in a few words, I would not even try, because that would oblige me to leave out key qualities that embody the man. One of the descriptors I would apply, however, to both Bob Miller and Nadine Hardin Miller, is "patriotic." Their mutual love for their country runs deep, yet they do not share the same politics. This makes for interesting discussions around the table about world matters, and issues like global warming, the economy, what's happening inside the Beltway in Washington, D.C., just how fake IS the news, and which cable channel to watch. As the earliest riser in the house, Bob gets to choose the channel for his morning serving of news, and it also entertains Nadine's beloved cat, Tiger, who has sincere affection for Bob. When I am at the Miller home, I am always glad to find my visit coinciding with the schedule for University of Arkansas sports. It doesn't matter if it's football or basketball, politics are secondary to the Razorbacks and mascots Sue E., Big Red, Boss Hog, Ribby and Pork Chop. Rooting for the home team comes first in the Miller household.

You might find it interesting that there is no mention of military service in the story, of this patriotic man who bleeds red, white and blue. Believe me, it's not due to lack of, or mediocre patriotism.

For younger readers who may not instantly recall the history lesson, our country once had a military draft. From 1948 until 1973, during both peacetime and eras of world conflict, men were drafted to fill vacancies in our military when there were not enough volunteers to sign up. The draft ended in 1973, and the U.S. converted to an all-volunteer military. Born in 1930, Bob was eligible for the draft at the age of 18.

The logistics of the draft followed this order — There was one drum containing birth dates January 1 through December 31, and another drum containing the sequence numbers from 1 through 365 (366 during a leap year). One capsule was drawn from each drum, and the date and number were paired to establish the sequence number for each birth date. This is done publicly so everyone would know the numbers. Men with the birth date drawn and with low lottery numbers were to report to the local recruitment office in town for a physical and assessment.

Before his number was ever drawn, Bob reported to the recruitment office to volunteer and sign up. At that time, the draft excluded men in college, so Bob was exempt. The next time Bob's birth date came up in the lottery, he went down to register. He was now married to Joanie and was told that he was not eligible due to being in college and married. The third notice sent Bob to the recruitment office again, only to find the draft excluded him because he was not only married, but now a father to Mike.

One afternoon, Bob called while he was driving home and said, "Jennifer, my nephew, Kip Vinson, has been making recordings of me talking about some of the highlights of my life, because he and his Dad thought it would be good for the family to have a book put together of my story; I guess they want it to pass on to future generations." Bob went on to say he was sure no one would want to read it, and that maybe a dozen books would suffice. He asked me if I would write his story.

By this time, I had heard more about Bob from other people than from Bob himself. What I had learned was intriguing, and I wanted to know more. I wanted to know what made him tick. The details were sparse and not attached to a relatable timeline. I believed if I was curious, others would also be interested, and piecing together Bob's story could create an accurate glimpse of the entirety of the man. Besides, who among us would not be curious about the secret of another's success, especially a person as successful as Bob Miller?

My first wise decision was to invite my friend, Nicholas Younes to get involved. Nicholas is a gifted, professional author, with extraordinary story-telling skills. I was confident he could help bring Bob's story to life. Nicholas traveled to Fort Smith and stayed in the Miller home to get to know Bob and Nadine as people, and to personally hear some of Bob's experiences. We hope the use of first person throughout this book allows you to hear Bob's story through him. Perhaps each of us will find a little of Bob Miller in our own lives. Spending time with him reconfigures one's thoughts, and fosters hope that his faith and great American dream will also be experienced by others.

Special thanks to Kip Vinson for sharing his recordings of conversations with Bob, as these proved invaluable to our process. Particular appreciation goes to Amanda Haynes for her fine editorial work.

JENNIFER TYLER

Dallas, Texas

May 28, 2019

FOREWORD

by Anne Mathews-Younes

My dear friend Bob Miller is a powerful example of the extraordinary role laity can play in the life of the church. Bob's spiritual mentor, E. Stanley Jones, always pointed to the significant contributions of the laity, and Bob was often Brother Stanley's prime example of an exceptional lay minister.

Bob lives the reality that the center of gravity in the Christian church is not the pulpit but the pew. When the church is pastor-centered the results will be largely rhetorical, but if it is lay centered, the output is always action. Listen to Bob's story about how he welcomed the mantle of lay minister: "E. Stanley Jones looked at me and told me something that completely changed my life. He said, 'Bob, all God wants is you, and if He has you, He will use you in whatever you choose to do. The Lord needs businessmen just as much as He needs preachers.'" Bob continues:

Meeting E. Stanley Jones gave me a sense of Ministry. I really believe that as I carried on as a drilling contractor in the Arkoma basin, I was performing ministry. I did my best to care for those around me and help anyone I came across, but more than this, I determined to be the best drilling contractor I could be, because God wanted it that way. In the days and years after my experience that God just wants me, I lived in unshakable faith that I was on the right path, and I believed that God would use me for the good and God has done so.

Consider the myriad of examples from Bob's life, where he consistently yokes his talents to his deepest beliefs to support to those in need. Bob traveled to Haiti to build wells and ensure clean drinking water for tens of thousands of Haitians. Consider Community Rescue Mission, the Mission in Fort Smith, Arkansas which, over the last 37 years, has cared for thousands of people and served more than 2,000,000 meals. The mission has offered a safe haven to help people get back on their feet. Today, the Mission focuses on instilling hope and empowering lives among families and children in crisis due to homelessness.

Bob's caring for others comes from a place of deep faith and prayer. He lives in the sure and certain knowledge that all of life is sacred and that every person can and ought to have a sense of mission. Bob lives the kind of life that proves you can put God into everything you do.

This story of Bob's life reminds us that "the most important question to answer in life is what we are going to do with Jesus." Walking with Jesus gave Bob the ministry he knew he needed. It has also made the appreciation of the blessings he has received so easy that, as he'll tell you, prayers of thanks fly up from him with almost every step he takes.

ANNE MATHEWS-YOUNES, ED.D., D.MIN.

Granddaughter of E. Stanley Jones
President, E. Stanley Jones Foundation

Anne and Bob, 2017

Oil painting by Gene Graham, capturing Bob's vocations and advocations

1

PROLOGUE

It was the end of a busy week. At last, it was Friday, a chance for a break. The social workers and nurses at the Edna Gladney Home were looking forward to the weekend. The temperature had not risen above 22 degrees, and there was talk of more snow with plummeting temperatures for the weekend.

Everyone was working long shifts. The Home was short-handed, and they were starting the new year with a few more moms and babies than they'd expected. Everybody was pitching in to get the job done. Some people on the evening shift were running late due to the icy road conditions, especially those driving into Fort Worth from the west. This meant nobody would be leaving on time.

The social worker was standing in the front hall when the door slowly opened. The figure of a young woman alone, carrying a bundle in her arms walked in hesitantly. Her steps were measured and unsure, as she glanced around, uncertain she was in the right place. This was a familiar scene to the staff, as the Edna Gladney Home welcomed many young mothers who brought their babies for trusted care and adoption. It was because of Mrs. Edna Gladney's work with the Texas State Legislature that Texas had one of the best and most developed adoption agencies in the country.

The young mother stopped in her tracks and reluctantly extended her arms toward an approaching social worker, who took the small bundle from her and gently placed it in an accompanying nurse's arms. One of the nurses said, "Get a warm blanket, the baby's hands are cold. Let's warm up those hands and take a look at what we have." She completely unfolded the blanket and said, "Oh, wow, look at those brown eyes. He is a charmer and with eyes like that, he will not be with us long. We have a bulging file of eager parents who would love to have this brown-eyed baby boy as their son."

While the Edna Gladney Home was the best option for young, unwed mothers who could not keep their babies, and for orphaned children, it was also a symbol of heartbreaking loss, the kind of loss that lingers in one's heart. After handing over her baby, the young mother disappeared into the administrative office, and after a time, she emerged sobbing, with her head bent low. She walked straight out the large door, down the frozen steps to the driveway, and fell into the front seat of a waiting car stopped with the motor running. The car's taillights cast a warm glow on the icy driveway as the car pulled away, never to return.

I have been told that as soon as I was born in Dallas the

man my mother hoped to marry drove her to the Edna
Gladney Home in Fort Worth with me in her arms. This was
where they placed me for adoption. After dropping me off,
they returned to Dallas and parted company. I can, at most,
imagine how long that drive must have seemed, the silence
broken only by my mother's sobs. That was the last she
would see of me or my biological father, the man she loved
and planned to marry. In their case, love didn't win as we see
in the movies. The three of us were supposed to be a family
and live happily ever after, but my biological grandfather's
social standing in the community, even during these
depression years, made that impossible.

There's a modicum of truth in how historians sometimes
characterize Texans during the depression years—as people
who didn't know there was depression on, let alone a *Great*
one. That platitude would be short lived, however. While
many people suffered monumental loss, others continued to
enjoy their standard of living due to the economic diversity of
the area, which included agriculture, cotton, and oil. It was
during the Depression that the extravagant Cotton Bowl
Stadium opened its doors at the State Fairgrounds in Dallas.

I have heard my biological grandfather was wealthy and
part of Dallas' high society, successful in business and owner
of a large cotton gin. I further suspect he gave his son, my
father, an ultimatum to "marry the girl and lose it all or walk
off." My father could not bear the thought of such a harsh
economic reality, so he drove me and my mother to Fort
Worth on that cold 10th day of January in 1930 and waited
outside in the car with the motor running, while my Mother
gave me up for adoption.

I believe my birth mother loved me dearly. I can only imagine her immense, heartfelt pain on the drive to the Edna Gladney Home, knowing what was ahead. I am thankful she had the fortitude to realize that without the support of my father, she could not provide for a baby at her young age. That unselfish act of giving me up for adoption is where my story really begins.

Edney Gladney Home with circle driveway, Circa 1930

2

TRIANGLE OF
EARLY LIFE

The great Depression took its toll across the country, and the Texas economy was not spared. Businesses and families were suffering. Jobs were very few and far between; even the proudest Texan had to acknowledge the depth of the economic crisis. The railroad, however, remained a bright spot. Railroads reached their peak in Texas in 1930 and, though they would gradually be replaced after World War II by trucks and cars, when I was born, the railroad was king. Even more importantly, the railroad was one of the few companies still hiring. The hours were long, and the pay was low, but people were glad to have a job.

Lester Eugene Miller was a locomotive engineer on the Fort Worth-Denver Line, which ran from Fort Worth through Wichita Falls, Childress, Amarillo, and Dalhart, to Texline. Les, as my dad was called, lived in Wichita Falls, Texas with his wife, Alice, and the railroad meant a steady job and a dependable paycheck for the couple. Les was from Chattanooga, Tennessee, and Alice was from Vernon, Texas. Les had a son by an earlier marriage, but he and Alice had no children. Alice badly wanted a baby boy to complete their family circle. She talked with Les about adoption, and she never gave up on her dream of one day having a son of their own.

Les worked long hours on the Fort Worth-Denver Railroad, and Alice was a homemaker. This gave her ample opportunity to do the necessary research about what adoption would entail. I can imagine Alice's eagerness to share the information she had gathered with Les, as they sat down to dinner. Over time, he came to understand the importance of a child to Alice, and agreed to adopt. Les loved Alice, and he wanted her to be happy.

In the 1930s, the average annual income was about $1,970. A locomotive engineer in the 1930s was paid about $0.55 an hour, which was good compensation during the depression. When Les did not work he was not paid, so he was always careful about the time he took off from work, and he took advantage of overtime as much as possible. Alice put their plans for adoption into motion; applications were completed and submitted, and the necessary background and home checks were done. Les and Alice were elated when they were approved for adoption. Les carefully planned for the day when he would need to take time off work to drive Alice the 118 miles from their home in Wichita Falls to Fort Worth, to make good on his promise to her. Work was extremely precious in those days and taking time off for a drive of that distance was no trivial matter.

Just about two weeks after my biological mother pushed open the front door of the Edna Gladney Home and handed me to the social worker; Alice and Les Miller walked through that same large door in the front hall to joyfully meet their brown-eyed baby boy.

They left for the journey back to Wichita Falls with me, wrapped snuggly in a warm blanket— a fresh, crisp birth certificate in hand bearing the name of their boy, Robert Eugene Miller, son of Lester Eugene and Alice Griggs Miller: born January 10, 1930. My short life's journey over those two weeks in January is a triangle that began in Dallas, traveled west to Fort Worth, and then turned north to Wichita Falls. I was on my way.

Bob and his Mother, Alice Miller

3

A PLACE TO CALL HOME

Long before Mom and Dad moved to Wichita Falls, Texas, the town residents had successfully induced the Fort Worth-Denver Railway Company to run the line through the town. The city offered the Railway substantial property concessions along the right-of-way and soon, with the arrival of the first train; an economic boom began.

By the time I arrived in my new hometown, Wichita Falls was well on its way to becoming a city and had a population of nearly 43,000 people. Schools, parks, churches, and retail establishments created a richness of life that was second to none, when compared to other small Texas towns.

Dad's work on the railroad was demanding. He provided well for our family, but this meant he had very little time off. He took me fishing when he could. You can't imagine how good it felt to have my father say, "Today we're goin' fishing." Those were the best days. Sometimes Mom and I would ride on the train when Dad was working. We'd sit in the back, to save the best seats for paying customers. I spent more time with my Mom than my Dad because of the schedule necessary to keep food on the table and a roof over our heads. I'm sure it comes as no surprise to folks of my generation, that I was closer to her than my Dad.

Mom kept watch over my education, but the sad truth of the matter was that I hated school. I could not bear the thought of sitting still all day in class and reading, not with so many enticements staring in at me from outside the school windows. I got through elementary school doing the minimum of what it took to pass, only because the thought of repeating a grade scared me more than the boredom of my lessons.

Dad never missed a paycheck during the Depression and that was by no means the case with other friends, neighbors and family. It was a blessing that I did not know how to appreciate fully as a young boy. It was Dad's job that kept it that way. We were by no means wealthy, but we were one of the few families with a steady, dependable job that allowed us to take vacations in the summer and maintain a comfortable lifestyle.

My parents were wonderful, kind, generous people who believed in helping others. They practiced what they preached. I remember there were a number of times my mother carried a meal down the street to one of her friends, or even to strangers. Growing up in that environment of generosity, as modeled by my parents, had a positive influence on me. I learned the value of a dollar and the importance of paying it forward and helping others.

My parents never hid the fact that I was adopted from me. There was a small plaque in my bedroom, which read, "You are Special because you were Chosen." My Mom said, "Of all the children in the world, we chose you to be our son." I knew I was loved, and I never felt isolated or alone. Mom would always include me in whatever she was doing. Watching her, I learned to prepare simple meals and do other chores around the house. She would say, "You'll make a great husband for some lucky girl one day."

As you might expect of good managers, my parents owned our home in Wichita Falls. The average cost of a house when I was born was around $7,000. The backyard at home was a kid's paradise, perfect for play. My friends and I would spend hours outside, where we could become anyone or anything we wanted to be, and transport ourselves as far as our imaginations could carry us. It was a wonderful place to grow up, with lots of sunshine and clean air. I haven't a doubt in my mind that it was the kind of place my Mom envisioned for her son when she and Dad bought the house.

No self-respecting Texas boy would want to be without a pair of cowboy boots and his own horse. My parents bought the lot beside our house and my Dad and I built a stall for my horse, Pet. I rode Pet as much as possible. Along with my bike, Pet was the main way I got around until I learned to drive.

The annual rodeo was a big deal in the county. People from surrounding counties would come with their horse trailers to participate in the rodeo prize events like barrel

racing, bronco and bull riding, roping and more. Grand
Entry was a parade up and down the front of the
grandstands, and a celebrated part of each day's opening
ceremonies. Every year, I saddled up Pet and we rode in the
Grand Entry. It was heady stuff, as a young boy, to be the
object of the loud cheers, and it was exhilarating. I felt like a
hero being welcomed back home after conquering the whole
world.

During my early elementary school years (we called it
grade school then), a view of my life resembled nothing so
much as a Norman Rockwell painting, expertly depicting a
happy, carefree boy and his dog. People nowadays might
find it hard to believe, but Norman Rockwell painted life as it
really was for some people. Small-town American life, as it
existed in Wichita Falls, may seem too good to have been
true, but I lived it, and I loved it, and its memory shines as
brightly today as life did back then.

When Dad did get a day off from work, we would
sometimes visit Mom's side of the family in Vernon, Texas,
which was then, about a thirty-minute ride. One weekend
there, my Dad took me to the Vernon flea market. The town
residents gathered on Saturday morning to sell, buy, and
trade everything from household goods to fresh vegetables,
clothing, farm equipment, furniture and more. If you could
imagine it, it was likely to be found there. The people were
friendly and eager to sell their wares. It was an awe-inspiring
place for a young boy, and I felt like an explorer searching for
hidden treasure. The hunt at the flea market far exceeded any
that my friends and I would conjure up in our backyard at
home. I didn't know exactly what I was searching for, but

that would soon become clear. I wasn't long into my exploration when I saw him, just sitting there. I know he saw me too by the way he was turning his head. He was watching my every move! It was love at first sight and the beginning of a friendship that would last for many years. He was the best dog I had ever seen. I was tickled when Dad, without hesitation, agreed to the adoption, paid the owner, and Smoky became the next four-legged, rag-tag, loved member of our family.

Smokey and I were inseparable. He was a gray fox-terrier with enough energy to keep up with my friends and me. Smoky never got tired waiting around for my friends and

Smokey looked like the dog in this photograph

me, and he was always ready to play his favorite game, fetch. He loved the backyard as much as we did. His high-pitched bark would signal the approach of a stranger, the discovery of a rodent outside, or just about anything else.

Dad drove a green Plymouth with wide running boards. He liked cars and traded them like clockwork every three years. When Mom, Dad, and I walked out the door of the house and headed for the car, Smoky would hop on the running board on the side of the car where I was sitting and go with us. He was always ready. Once Smoky was planted securely on the running board, he had perfect balance. Neither speed, bumpy roads nor curves posed a threat to him. There was just no way Smokey was going to be dislodged, thrown off, or worst of all, left behind. He and I were best friends well into my high school years.

Dad's appreciation for cars, as well as his good sense to always pay cash for them made an impression on me. Like Dad, there are few things I love more than cruising down the road, particularly if it's in my own car. I made it my rule to pay cash for my cars, from my first car purchase in high school all the way down to the Hyundai Equus I drive today. Always pay cash for cars. It gives you the competitive edge to negotiate the best price.

4

THE FARM

In April of each year I would pull out a calendar and begin marking off the days until classes ended for the summer. Summer was freedom from being cooped-up in a classroom and homework assignments, and summer held the promise of playing with Smokey as much as I could. Summer also meant I would have more time to spend with my friends. Best of all, each summer we would take our annual trip to Chattanooga to visit my Dad's family. Because Dad was a locomotive engineer, we could get free railway passes for all of our trips, provided the destinations were serviced by Dad's railway line. The week we were to leave, Dad made sure our tickets were in order and Mom worked feverishly to get things ready to go. I couldn't wait to board the train, and my mind was filled with all the fun I would have once we arrived. The hardest part was leaving Smokey behind in the trusted care of one of my friends.

We boarded the train for Tennessee, and I was eager to find a window seat. Though I could hardly wait to get to the Tennessee farm, once I boarded the train, I was captivated by the steady, slight rocking of the train and clicking of the wheels on the rail, tapping out a music of expectation. While Mom and Dad relaxed and settled into their seats, I was a more than enthusiastic spectator, thoroughly engaged by what flew past outside my window from my carefully selected perch. Anybody who has looked out an airliner's window (or passenger train window) and seen a great city knows what I felt. I could see it all, and anything beyond my line of vision I could imagine. Roadrunners, coyote, and deer were frequent sightings, as the train sped along the way. Though I kept my eyes peeled for a bear as we traveled through Tennessee, I never saw one. As the flat lands surrounding Wichita Falls gave way to the rolling hills, and ultimately the lush valleys and emerald lakes along the route, the sharpness of the cloud formations across the mountains was spectacular and seemed individually painted by some unseen hand. Each held a lesson in natural science, beyond the classroom, and the makings of great stories to share with my cousins.

We stayed with my Dad's family on a farm just outside of Chattanooga. They always had their three grandchildren at the farm when we were there. As an only child, I had no preparation for the constant companionship of other kids one experiences in a large family. My cousins gave me an inside view of what life was like with siblings. Life lessons were abundant each summer with my extended siblings. I took crash courses in how to bargain hard and daily lessons in how to get my two cents in when significant decisions were under consideration. Each day, there were important choices to make — should we go fishing first and swim later or swim before fishing? The ends might seem trivial, but let me tell you, there is nothing children take more seriously than the discussions they have about which way to have fun.

There was a river on the back border of the farm and every day we'd make a beeline for it. It had clear, cold water with a mild current that moved it along its rocky bottom. It was the best place to fish for miles around. Sometimes we could see the fish swimming just below the surface, as though daring us to try to catch them. The farm and river were the part of my childhood that edged out of Norman Rockwell and into Mark Twain. Fishing and swimming always headed our daily list of things to do. On the days we got lucky, and the fish were biting, we would race back to the house, trophies in hand, and my grandmother would cook the fish for us. Those were the most tender, juiciest fish I have ever eaten to this day. It is amazing how childhood memories from eighty years ago can cause the food of the best chefs in the most exclusive restaurants in the world to pale by comparison.

My cousins had chores to do each day. I would help them take care the chickens, cows, and horses. It never seemed like work when we fed and watered the livestock. I enjoyed the responsibility to preserve the life of the animals who depended on us. The school my cousins attended was in the country, just down the road from the farm. They walked to school most of the time. One of my cousins and I shared a mutual dislike for school. He would frequently hide under the bed, hoping his absence would go unnoticed, as the other kids left for school. I knew that trick would never work at my "only-child" house, and it didn't work for him either. According to my aunt, only the threat and fear of bodily harm could persuade him out from under the bed for school. From his vantage point under the bed, he was safe and free, but all he got for his trouble was a little dust on his clothes, because he still had to go to class despite his disappearance. My aunt, on the other hand, got the best deal. Her son was educated, and she never once had to dust the wood floor under his iron bed during the academic year.

The farm was also the place where I had my first opportunity to work an "angle" that held the potential for a very favorable outcome. I was in high school at the time, and my cousin who was close to my age, arranged dates for us one weekend. Back then we called that a double date. Now days, it seems kids just hang out in groups. We were very excited about going out with real live girls—sisters to boot. My cousin and I made plans that we hoped they would enjoy, and we could hardly wait for the weekend.

If you ask a person who lives in Tennessee where he or she is from, the frequent answer will be "I'm from... East Tennessee, Middle Tennessee or West Tennessee." There are good reasons for this distinction. Natural boundaries separate the state and create distinctive terrains, economies, and lifestyles. The Appalachian and Smokey Mountain ranges characterize East Tennessee. The majestic Cumberland Plateau and the Tennessee Valley separate East from Middle Tennessee. West Tennessee, on the other hand, is rich, flat agricultural land bound by the Tennessee River on the east and the Mississippi river on the West. Middle and West

Tennessee are in the Central Time Zone. The farm and the girls we were dating were in East Tennessee, and the Eastern Time Zone. This fact was important to my strategic "angle," or so I thought.

We took the girls to a movie and then to the local burger and shake shack. We were having a great time, just talking and enjoying our vanilla shakes, when suddenly we realized the curfew for the girls was getting close. The evening was just beginning! It was at that moment I realized how close we were to the line of demarcation between the Central and Eastern time Zones. My cousin and I figured we could squeeze out an extra hour to spend with our dates by taking the girls across the time zone, where it was an hour earlier. That would give us plenty of time to work up our courage to kiss-em. The girls didn't seem to mind. Unfortunately, I cannot say the same for their Father; my brilliant exploitation of Central Standard Time cut no ice with him. When we took the girls home, he let us know, in no uncertain terms, that the only time that mattered was the time showing on his clock, and by its face, we were one hour late! I took his stern lecture to heart, but it did not dull the experience of the evening, especially my first kiss in the Central Time Zone!

I learned that when you think you have considered all the pros and cons related to your strategy, it is best to talk it over with an unbiased friend, to see if your "angle" is plausible.

The free railway passes were a perk that made our trip to Tennessee doable for Mom, Dad, and me to get away most summers until my high school years. There were no interstate highways in those days and without the train, our 1,000-mile road trip to the farm would have been absolutely impossible.

When there was little to see out the window, I was happily engaged in games, comic books, crossword puzzles and enjoying some of the delicious snacks Mom packed for the trip. To my credit, I learned to resist asking, "Are we there yet?"

My cousins and I packed a lot of memories into those two weeks. It was at the farm in Tennessee, that I discovered my enduring love and appreciation for the great outdoors beyond my own backyard in Wichita Falls, my enjoyment of the farm animals, and numerous other life lessons. Among the most important lessons I learned was that the time zone angle does not impress, as an excuse for being late!

Bob and his Dad, Les Miller

5

FINDING MY WAY

When asked about my childhood, I would frequently say I had a wonderful, uneventful childhood, filled with love and adventure. In the turmoil and uncertainty of today's world, and the contribution it made to my life, I have come to appreciate the depth of that tranquility. I never thought much about the support and encouragement my family gave me, but thankfully, my gratitude surfaced as I matured. It was the decade of the Great Depression, yet my parents always found a way to keep me involved in scouting and sports. In our household, while Dad earned money in locomotives, Mom worked twice as hard keeping the home fires burning and her family running like a well-oiled machine. I enjoyed life.

There were no TVs or smart phones when I was a boy, only radios. I usually went to bed early, and I was an early riser. As the aroma of fried eggs and bacon wafted through the hall, into my bedroom, it made it easy for me to hop out of bed and get going for the day. I could always count on Mom to serve me breakfast, with a big glass of cold milk, delivered fresh each day by the neighborhood milkman.

Since modern refrigerators were uncommon in homes until after World War II, Mom had an icebox that required a delivery of a large block of ice to keep our food cold. There was a drip pan in the bottom of the icebox to catch the liquid from the melting ice, which would be emptied daily. Ice was sold by the pound, so it was important for Mom to put the sign in the front window to let the delivery man know how much she wanted to buy, (25, 50, 75, or 100 pounds). Sometimes the blocks of ice were wrapped in old newspaper to help postpone its melting.

Vintage window sign for ice delivery

Smokey would hear the squeaky breaks and signal us with his shrill bark that the delivery truck was coming our way. The truck was still slowly rolling when the "swamper," as he was called, would glide down from his seat, with unbroken rhythm, grab the correct weight of ice with a large pair of hooked tongs, then gracefully balance it on a square of burlap strapped to his shoulder, and jump out the back of the truck. He would walk into our kitchen and deposit the ice in the icebox. It was impressive, and the kind of customer service one can only dream of today.

When I was in middle school, I decided to try my hand at delivering ice too. I could fit it into my schedule in the morning without interfering with after school work. Besides, if I could hoist the blocks of ice on my shoulder like our swamper, it would be a work-out program to build muscle, judging from the breadth of the iceman's shoulders.

Three things stand out about my short career as an ice swamper — biting dogs, injury, and that appearances deceive. I knew where every fierce, biting dog lived on my route. If the owner wanted ice, milk or any other deliveries, the dog had to be leashed or tied to a tree or post to protect the deliveryman from harm. I learned quickly to estimate the length of the rope used to tie-up the biting dogs, so I could walk a wide circle around that dog. Secondly, on the job accidents happen swiftly. Once the ice tongs I was using slipped off the block of ice, sailed through the air, hit my driver in the face and broke his tooth. He just kept on driving through the pain. I felt terrible about it when it happened, and I still do. Last, the swamper's well practiced, effortless grace made lofting those blocks appear far easier than it was.

Newspapers, radio, and movie shorts (then called 'newsreels') were the only ways of keeping up with the news. The golden age of radio's popularity was in the 1930s and 1940s. The economic and political scenes here at home were in turmoil, and soon millions of Americans had gone off to fight in World War II. President Franklin D. Roosevelt's "New Deal" of public works created jobs and brought some relief. If the Great Depression wasn't enough, the Dust Bowl began to ravage the Great Plains. There was no shortage of world and national news. I could not follow everything the newscasters were reporting, but we talked about some of the headlines in school.

We had one radio in our house. Every evening Mom and Dad were eager to hear the news. Many a family who could not afford payments on their washing machines or Model A Ford's, struggled mightily to keep current on payments for their radios. Visualize this: some of the radios then were huge extravagant pieces of lovely, carved furniture, elegantly placed in a drawing room. Knowing that, makes it a little easier to understand how keeping up a monthly payment on such a significant item could be a problem, when most of the working people were jobless. Our radio, however, was nondescript, and there was nothing fancy about it.

Mom, Dad, and I often listened to the radio together. Once Mom and Dad finished listening to the news, Mom would switch over to one of a wide range of programs that included music, comedy, quiz shows, and dramatic productions. The most celebrated radio show when I was growing up was the Lux Radio Theater, performed live on stage in front of a studio audience. It lasted an hour and starred famous

Hollywood personalities who plugged Lux Soap during intervals, which did not impress me. I preferred the Lone Ranger and Tonto. It was shorter, and I thought it was a much better use of my time. Mom and Dad sometimes listened to George Burns. He could always make them laugh. On Saturday and Sunday nights, we all enjoyed the Music Hall of Fame. Hank Williams, the Grand Ole Opry, Bob Wells and his Western Swing band, and country-western music were universal favorites.

Every Sunday, barring interruptions by illness or vacation, my family and I were seated at our spots on the pew in the sanctuary of Grace Methodist Church in Wichita Falls. Like most families in town, the church was the center of our social life. We were involved with neighbors in whatever the church was doing, whether extending a helping hand to those in need in Wichita Falls, holding special prayer meetings to petition the Lord with concerns, or other events sponsored by the congregation. If you have ever been part of a Methodist church, you know the congregation is filled with church ladies who are great cooks, including my Mom, and we frequently enjoyed meals together as a church family in the fellowship hall.

Grace Methodist Church was the place where seeds of faith were planted into my life that would later germinate and take root. I became an official member of the congregation at ten years old, when confirmed by our minister. Grace Methodist was where I sang in the choir "Jesus loves me this I know for the Bible tells me so" and the truth of that statement continues undiminished with me today. Later, the church relocated to Taft Blvd, across from

Mid-Western University and changed its name to University United Methodist Church. In 1997, the church was refurbished and expanded. I returned to the church for a special service to express my gratitude and honor my parents, Les and Alice Miller, by dedicating the chancel rail in their memory.

The war became real to me beyond radio news when Sheppard Military Base was built outside of Wichita Falls, and the soldiers began coming into town. Some had been wounded in the line of duty, and others were at the base awaiting orders to be deployed. We usually brought one or two soldiers home with us from church to share our Sunday lunch. Mom was a good cook, and her Sunday meals became well known through town, even in an era when most women knew how to lay out large meals.

The war altered life for everyone. Mom and Dad were more keenly aware of its inconveniences than me. Rationing was an everyday occurrence. Coupons and stamps were given to citizens to regulate quantities of gasoline, sugar, food, and many other items that could previously be purchased without limit. A large amount of food was being shipped overseas to feed the troops, and it was important to control waste of vital commodities back home. Domestic production requiring rubber and steel was curtailed to ensure equipment could be manufactured and available for our soldiers in battle. The impact could even be felt in the clothing industry. Cotton, for example, was no longer available for making civilian clothes because every yard of it was needed to go into military uniforms.

The soldiers became real people to us, not just distant

figures in a news story. They sat at our table, shared stories of the people they loved and left at home; moms, dads, siblings, wives, and children, and they talked about what it was like back home. They made the war personal to us, made us see that these men were fighting for their families, in addition to the Nation, and we could easily see the toll it took on them. Home cooking, a cozy welcoming living room, and friendly conversation provided an appreciated escape for them, if only for the afternoon.

My elementary school years were marked by less than stellar scholastic achievements. As it was to many boys my age, recess was the best time of the school day. It didn't take my friends and me long to race to the baseball field for a quick game. Each of us played more than one position, depending on who could show up that day. We would play hard and fast to make the most of the time we had. The most annoying sound that ever came out of that school, was the ringing of the bell when my team was trailing by one, and the bases loaded. Like it or not, our unfinished studies could not be ignored, even for a single base hit to even up the score.

Once I officially earned the rite of passage from elementary to middle school, Mom exercised her authority over my education and moved me to a new middle school across town, in a more affluent part of the city. The middle school there had a reputation for quality academics, and Mom wanted to make sure I was scholastically challenged so I could realize my potential. Much to Mom's disappointment, the new school did not instill in me the excitement and love for the classroom she expected.

I joined the Boys' Club of America and hoped I could find

my place among my peers. The Boys' Club of America provided a wholesome environment where boys could learn different skills, play various kinds of sports, and just have plain fun. It provided a group of fast friends who took the edge off being the new kid.

I was never a large guy, compared to my friends and other boys in my school. I did not have a line-backer physique, so it didn't make sense for me to go out for the football team. No doubt some of the football boys thought of me as a sissy. One day, the football boys decided they were going to have a boxing match and they picked me as the opponent to box the team quarterback. This guy was huge. He was a powerhouse, and even more muscular than our "swamper". He lifted weights and ate at the coach's training table. No one could get past him on the football field. He plowed through everything in sight. He significantly outweighed me and had a reputation for being tougher than nails. The football team was good, in large part, because of the quarterback's brawn. Football games were a town-wide affair that emptied the streets. We Texans took our high school football seriously then, and we still do now. "Friday Night Lights" all the way.

News of the unequally matched boxing event traveled, and it drew quite a crowd. However, the match did not end as anticipated. Little did that quarterback know he would be facing a lean, mean machine who'd learned to box and honed his skills at the Boys' Club. The quarterback hardly laid a hand on me. I knocked him to the floor, and before he knew what hit him, he fell to his knees. From then on, I gained brand new respect and found a friend in my defeated opponent, the quarterback. That was a memorable day. The element of surprise can give you the upper hand, wait for it, and use it to your advantage.

I continue to value the work of the Boys' Clubs of America today because I know it makes a difference in the lives of youth when it is most needed. I serve on their board in Fort Smith, Arkansas, and support their work anyway I can.

Bob and Nadine on a cruise

6

VENTURING OUT

By 1940, Wichita County had become Texas's most active oil county, having produced 320,000,000 barrels of oil. Agriculture, cattle, and farming were economic powerhouses that swelled the population of my home town to near 100,000 by 1940.

My parents instilled a strong work ethic in me, and they suggested it would be good for me to get a job. They were right. I was working steadily at various jobs throughout middle and high school, as my class schedule permitted. I was selling newspapers in 1941 at the tender age of 11. I remember well the insatiable appetite of the townspeople for the latest news in the wake of the Japanese attack on Pearl Harbor. I was standing on the corner in Wichita Falls, papers in hand, shouting "Extra, Extra, Read all about it! Japanese Attack on Pearl Harbor." That was a shocking day for Mom and Dad, our friends and neighbors, and our country. It was also my first inkling that world events actually do impact the economy. That day, I could not keep enough newspapers to sell, and I made a lot of money. I also sold magazines from building to building. The most popular money makers for me were *The Saturday Evening Post, Readers Digest, and Collier's Magazine.*

When I wasn't selling newspapers or magazines, I was delivering drugstore prescriptions on my bicycle after school. It was cheaper for the drugstore owner to hire me to make the deliveries, than to hire someone with a car. I was glad to get the work. Besides, he liked the fact that I was dependable and always on time.

With my brief career as an ice swamper over, I took a job at a seasonal stand that sold cold watermelon slices. It wasn't a long-term job, but it paid me well as a younger worker. We would cut the watermelon slices and lay them out on the tables. It may sound like an inconsequential job, but when the temperatures in July and August climbed above 100° for days on end, those watermelon slices sold faster than we could cut them on sweltering summer evenings.

One night the man who owned the watermelon business got drunk and left early. On his way out, he told me to take the watermelon delivery truck home, so the melons could be delivered the next day. At age 13, I didn't know how to drive, but by the time I got home, I could shift the gears. The next morning my Mother awoke to see the truck outside and thought someone was in our driveway. I said, "No Mom, I drove the truck home last night." She could not believe what I was saying and exclaimed, "What! Bob, you are too young to drive, and you don't have a license." I further explained it was the owner's idea for me to drive the truck home. I didn't say anything about the owner partying too hard the evening before.

I learned to drive officially when I was 14, and it revolutionized my ability to deliver groceries. Though I couldn't get a license until I was 16, I drove the grocery store owner's truck to make the deliveries. He didn't mind my driving, provided I didn't have a wreck. He knew the truck made it possible for me to give even better customer service, and I saw the value of that in my tips. The ability to drive the truck extended my delivery territory. I could venture farther out into the more affluent neighborhoods of Wichita Falls. There, I saw for the first time how the "other" half lived.

Our vacations to the farm in Chattanooga were less frequent in my high school days. Summertime was now the season for work. Three summers while in high school, I worked on ranches in the Texas Panhandle. I dated a girl whose Dad owned a small ranch, which adjoined a very large ranching operation in West Texas of more than a hundred sections. Given that a section of land is one square mile (640 acres), that was a sizeable ranch by anyone's standards. Her brother, Leslie, and I were friends, so he got the job for me. Many of the regular cowboys were in the armed services that summer, so it was easier for me to find work. That large ranching operation offered all kinds of opportunities for me to learn, from herding and branding cattle to breaking horses. We worked long hours and at night I bedded down in a huge bunk house designed for a dozen or more ranch hands, surrounded by empty bunks.

The rancher had 12 two-year old colts, which had to be broken. The colts had no intention of being ridden by anyone, let alone a wiry little cowpoke like me. I was no horse whisperer, but I had grit. There, I learned all aspects of ranching, including how to ride bucking horses. That experience would later serve me well. I worked on that large ranch for two summers before moving to a smaller ranch. When I was on the ranch, I was in my element — I was outdoors and doing what I loved. I became a good rancher, if I do say so myself.

I loved animals so much that I tried my hand at the rodeo. When you're eighteen years old, nothing seems impossible. Success is guaranteed, and not only can you not fail, but there's nothing you won't try. This came pretty naturally to me because one of my jobs on the ranch was to break horses that had never been ridden. First, I would get one of the two-year old colts and carefully strap a saddle to his back. Then, I'd keep my distance as he tried to buck the saddle off until he finally accepted it. After that, and this seems crazy to everybody who hears it, I would carefully climb into that saddle and let the horse try and buck me off. I stayed glued to that saddle, as if my life depended on it, riding that wild horse for as long as it would take for him to realize he couldn't shake me. I stayed put, no matter what. When the horse tried to reach back and bite me, or rear up and fall over backwards with me on his back, I just held on for dear life! It didn't take me long to develop a quick set of reflexes when I had only half of a second to get from between the horse and the ground to avoid being crushed, if the colt decided to flip over. Imagine doing that 12 times a day, and it works up a big appetite.

While working on the ranch I would have weekends to myself. I joined the collegiate rodeo team with a few friends, and on Saturdays we would head into the small towns in the area where we could always find the rodeo. I aspired to become a bull rider. My days on the ranch gave me plenty of experience to develop my skills. At the weekend rodeos, local ranchers would bring in three of the liveliest bulls from their ranches to enter the rodeo. Now granted, these were not the kind the bulls you might see on the rodeo circuit today, professional bulls, but they were a challenge for me back then. There's plenty of a challenge in a docile bull who gets his ginger up when he's got a strap round him for the first time. On one particular weekend, I went to a rodeo south of Amarillo, Texas. That rodeo was at its best, with a huge crowd from all over the county and livestock that appeared better than usual. My friends and I got there early to pay our entry fees and size up the bulls. They looked big, mean and ready to take on any rider who dared to mount them. When my time came, my bull was ready for me. I managed to stay on him long enough to win a respectable third place and $40 in the bull riding contest. Luckily, it only took one experience of a bull's horn coming straight for me to make me realize that college held more of a future for me than riding bulls. That was further confirmed after I subtracted my entry fee and expenses from my prize money.

Working on a ranch is a full-time job, and we would frequently pull long hours cutting hay, running cattle or any number of other demanding — and dusty — tasks. My friend

Leslie was working with me one day, driving the tractor. Typically, Leslie would lift the equipment carriage at the end of a row with his foot planted solidly on the tractor, make a wide turn, and head back in the opposite direction, and release the carriage to do its work. On this particular day, when he made the turn, his foot was not on the tractor, but dangling from it when he lifted the carriage. His dangling foot was crushed between the tractor axle and the carriage lift.

Leslie was writhing in excruciating pain, and I quickly loaded him in my truck and headed for the emergency room at the nearest hospital. Thankfully, he did not have to wait long for treatment. When a nurse walked into his room with a large syringe filled with medicine for his pain Leslie started loudly begging, "Oh no, oh God no, not a shot, please no shot, please no, please"! Standing beside his bed, I could see the level of pain he was in, and I thought, what on earth could be more horrible and painful than a crushed foot? Evidently, Leslie thought the fright and pain of the needle trumped everything!

Mom and Dad did not seem to mind my summer ranch occupations. They knew I was learning useful, practical things, and the work boosted my savings. Even as a young man in the rapidly booming domestic economy, the lessons of the Depression loomed. I saved virtually every cent I earned as a ranch hand.

My preteen and teenage years were marked by extraordinary technological advances and inventions most people could not live without today. Just imagine running your household without shiny, grey duct tape or a microwave or babysitting your grandchild without disposable diapers or taking care of your cat without kitty litter. Aviation, electronics, radar, Penicillin and more, opened the floodgate for continued, amazing progress. Television made its debut, and was quickly followed by color television. The first passenger air service across the Atlantic began.

We had a telephone in our house, but it was nothing like today. It could have been quite entertaining if it weren't so exasperating. Rather than the private line we know today, we had a party line, and the more people sharing the line, the merrier. Several families shared one trunk line to form the party line. Each family was assigned a distinctive ring, and everyone on the party line could hear one another's ring. When we received a call, it was common for neighbors to pick up the telephone and listen in on our conversation. Mom always told me never to say anything on the phone you didn't want to see in the headlines. She was correct, and even more accurate as the 20th century turned into the 21st.

A few of the neighbors were more intrusive than others, and it was usually easy to figure out who was listening in, based on the background noise in their home. A simple "hang up, we are on the phone" hardly deterred the uninvited listeners. When the private line was offered, my parents wasted no time in signing up.

The telephone book was a staple in every home, an encyclopedia of names, addresses and numbers for people within the local area. The phone book was displayed in a prominent location and carried inside it, hand-written notes for new contact information for businesses, friends, and family as needed. By the time the new "phone book" came out, our old one was filled with important notations. Today, phone books are largely obsolete, and their value is more for the pizza discount coupons inside the cover. Recently, I went to get a new cell phone. Within minutes, my contacts, phone numbers, and pictures populated my new phone with no effort from me. It was exactly the sort of miracle many people today cannot fully appreciate.

Though the first aircraft, a Bleriot XI Monoplane, made its debut in Wichita Falls in 1912, when I was a boy, airplanes were still a fascinating mystery. I remember a news article that said an airplane was coming to Wichita Falls before the airfield was built. One of the town's people owned a flat piece of land and worked a deal with a company in Dallas to fly an airplane to Wichita Falls and land it. The populace turned out in droves to see the plane. If a person had the money for a ticket — and was not afraid — he or she could go up in the plane that very day.

I was in the crowd, watching in awe as a few people stepped up, paid for the ticket and boarded the plane. Each one waved good-bye to friends and family when boarding. It was the most exciting thing I had seen since I first laid eyes on Smokey at the Vernon, Texas flea market.

The door of the plane closed, and the engines revved up, preparing the plane for takeoff. There was a fence around the flat property where the plane landed and was now beginning to taxi. I remember thinking, "I hope there is a gate at the end of that strip of land, otherwise, how in the world will the plane be able to take off?" It turns out, there was no gate, and the plane did not need one anyway. It slowly rose over the trees, soaring above the clouds, evoking a gasp and cheer from those of us left behind, some of whom were digging in pockets for the price of a ticket.

It was many years later before I had the chance to take my first plane ride as an adult, but ever since that moment I have loved flying and been entranced by its mystery.

Mike and Lori (Nadine's daughter and son-in-law) with Nadine and Bob

7

ENTREPRENEURS
IN TRAINING

Jimmy Doolen and I were fast friends; we clicked from the first moment we met. We understood each other implicitly and always had each other's backs. Everybody needs a friendship like the one I had with Jimmy. It bridged the gap between junior high and high school, often a graveyard of childhood friendships, and it continued into our adult years.

Throughout the time I was steadily working, I was saving my money. I had $50 to show for my labor. Fifty dollars in 1941 had the same buying power as $890 in 2019. Once Jimmy and I decided to partner together to buy our first car, we hit the big time. We needed $100 to make our first deal and the car would be ours. I had my $50 saved and ready, but Jimmy had to go to work to earn his $50. We paid $100 for an old Model-A Ford. Originally, it was a convertible, but there wasn't anything left of the rag top to confirm that. Nevertheless, we owned a convertible, and Jimmy and I cruised about town in our car with pride. The Model-A was manufactured from 1929 through 1931. We bought our red beauty in 1946. It was hot, the muscle car of the day, or at least that's how Jimmy and I saw it.

Some people warned Jimmy and me that going into business as friends would ruin our friendship. That never happened with us. We never had a cross word. We both drove the car and agreed to a plan. Whoever's home we were closest to by nightfall would hop out, and the other would drive the car home. The next day whoever was driving the car would loop by to pick up the other one for school. It worked like a charm.

1930 Model A Ford Convertible like Bob and Jimmy
bought, minus the convertible top.

Jimmy and I had an eye for fancy hubcaps, and the fancier the better. I am not saying how, but from time to time, some of these fancy hubcaps fell into our hands. We would either put them on our car to enjoy and attract attention or sell them for a nice price to other hubcap aficionados.

Eventually, we sold our first car and doubled our money. With the profit, we paid cash for our next car investment. We bought and sold cars all through high school. We were much more passionate about our cars than our classes.

Even with our success as entrepreneurs, Jimmy and I had a grand plan for our lives beyond buying and selling cars.

Robert (Bob) Miller

8

THE FIRST GRAND PLAN

Jimmy Doolen's Dad owned the town drug store. Jimmy and I thought about following in his footsteps and becoming pharmacists. That career seemed to work out well for his father. We might even take over the drug store in the future. After much conversation, Jimmy and I agreed we would go to pharmacy school. I was pretty sure Mom and Dad had been saving money for my college, and I had been saving too. I knew college would be expensive, and merit scholarships were clearly off the table for me.

Jimmy's family had more money than mine, so he planned to go to Oklahoma University. I was headed to Hardin Junior College. After graduation from Wichita High, Jimmy and I were on our way to fulfill our grand plan. Since he was leaving for Norman, Oklahoma and Oklahoma University, it seemed right for me to buy out his share of the

Studebaker car we owned at the time. I could use the car to get to and from classes and work. I kept that car until the end of my freshman year at college.

Truthfully, I was getting sick and tired of repairing and flipping old cars, and ironically, I was stuck with one. I *wanted* a new car. I was *ready* for a new car. I *deserved* a new car. I talked to my Dad about it and he said, "Bob, your Mom and I have been saving money to send you to college, and we have $2,000. Now, you can either use that money to buy yourself a new car, or you can use it to go to college." With numerous jobs and ranching experience under my belt, I was feeling confident of my ability to support myself financially and pay my own way through school. I was always earning money in some way. I tried to look wise and sound mature when I said, "Dad, I'll take the car!"

First new car, including the new car
smell, 1947 Plymouth

A new car was just the incentive I needed. There is nothing like the new-car smell. It is intoxicating, an aroma that becomes imprinted in one's mind, to be recalled at will. I went down to the Plymouth dealership to try out my negotiation skills. There were not many options or bells and whistles in those days to obscure the real price. I ended up paying about $1700 for my first new car, a 1947 Plymouth. I was soaring with satisfaction and delight. I owned a new car! After the deal, I still had a nice little nest egg of $300 to start saving toward my next car. Buying my first car was a valuable experience. I learned one important thing that day. The dealer had a markup of 25%. Knowing the dealer's markup positions you to make the best deal. My first new car was worth every cent I paid, and the education was valued at even more. It was the kind of lesson that keeps on giving.

I was partial to Ford cars, and after driving the Plymouth for a while, I decided to trade it in on a blue 1950 Ford. Knowing the markup, I started my negotiation offer at 5% above wholesale cost. The salesman was shocked at my offer and said, "Oh no, we could never accept that." As I turned walking away, he stopped me and continued the conversation. Eventually, we settled on 12% above wholesale and made a deal-or so he thought. At that precise moment, I used the most effective weapon in my negotiation quiver. I said, "How much for cash?" This saved me another $50. Thanks Dad, for the important lesson to pay cash for cars. Always remember, salesmen rarely let a live-one get away and timing is everything.

My Dad died when I was eighteen. He was always there when I needed him, and a real father to me. I wish he could have lived longer and been a part of my life in my adult years. Even though I was young, I always knew Dad was proud of me.

It only took me one semester at Hardin Junior College to learn my destiny would not include an indoor job as a pharmacist. The farm in Chattanooga and working on the ranches in West Texas had confirmed my love and appreciation for the outdoors. I needed to feel the sun on my skin and the wind against my face, to see a daybreak outside and sunset at the end of the day. About the same time, Jimmy came to the realization that college was not for him. He dropped out of Oklahoma University and headed home. It was good to have him back in town, but I knew important life decisions awaited both of us. We resumed our friendship with ease, and we continued working.

I decided to pursue a degree in animal husbandry at Midwestern College. I loved animals and wanted to be outdoors, and this seemed like a degree that offered career options upon graduation. I was among the first graduates the year Midwestern became a University.

9

WINDS OF CHANGE

I was living on the college farm helping to take care of the livestock. A graduating senior had the job of artificial inseminator of dairy cattle for Wichita County. After graduation, he could no longer keep the job. It had to go to another student, and the job became mine. The ranchers and farmers could hire the college to inseminate their dairy cows more cheaply than it cost to pay stud fees. When the cattle saw my truck coming down the dusty road, it caught their attention; they knew I was headed there for them. The job paid me well, and I could coordinate it nicely with my classes.

One day Jimmy and I were driving through the Country Club neighborhood, admiring the beautiful homes. (From time to time, my Dad and I traveled that same route, and he admired the homes and wondered what it would be like to be financially able to live there.)

Suddenly, I saw a girl in the front yard of 2208 Maranda Street. I had driven by that big white house many times when I made deliveries, but I had never seen that girl before. Jimmy didn't know her either. We both thought she was beautiful. Right then and there, I declared to Jimmy that I was going to date her, though I didn't know her name! I think Jimmy was amused by my confidence, but he of all people should know that when I set my mind to something, I see it through.

All week I was still thinking about that girl we saw on the lawn. Thankfully, one of our friends had a party and invited Jimmy and me. My lucky stars were shining bright that night, because who should walk in but the girl I saw at 2208 Maranda. I found out her name was Joan Vinson. Her friends called her Joanie. I learned she had been attending the Hockaday School in Dallas, an expensive school reserved only for those who could afford the tuition. Her parents, Helen and Jerry Vinson, wanted her to go to the exclusive prep school, and Joanie agreed to go with the understanding that she could return to Wichita Falls High for her senior year.

My plan to date Joanie was diverted, but not for long. Soon after the party, Billy Bob Wolfe and I had a double date with Jean Douglas and Joanie Vinson. Billy Bob was with Joanie, and I was with Jean. By the time the evening was over, I was with Joanie and he was with Jean. That started our courtship.

Dating Joanie created angst for her mother, Helen. Joanie's mother knew me as the kid who brought groceries or pharmacy items to her friends in the neighborhood. She was not happy her daughter was dating the delivery boy. She thought I was just interested in Joanie because she was from a well-to-do family. I honestly believe she continued thinking that until I sold my company the day I turned 50 years old.

Joanie's Dad and I always had a good relationship. Jerry grew up in the humble beginnings in Sweetwater, Texas. He came to Wichita Falls, got a job and became very successful with his own supply business. It started out as a partnership and he ended up buying out his partner. I think he appreciated the fact that I was hard-working. It says a lot about a man if he can see his own best features in others less fortunate.

It didn't take long for Joanie and me to become serious about one another. We enjoyed each other's company and looked forward to going to drive-in movies, dances, and seeing friends. I was going to college at the time, and Joanie was a senior in high school. We were not dating anyone else, and everyone who knew us could see we were serious about a future together.

Money was always an issue for me, and I never planned anything for us to do without first thinking about how much it would cost. Sometimes Joanie would drive to the college farm where I was working, in her mother's yellow convertible. She had two speeds, full-throttle and motionless. I could see her coming for a mile, barreling down the road, kicking up a rooster tail of dust. She would sit on the fence and watch me work with the cattle. I'm sure she never learned anything like that at Hockaday.

It was common knowledge among the society set that

Helen Vinson wanted to give her daughter a huge, glorious wedding, appropriate to the family's standing. The thought of this loomed over our courtship and was a topic of frequent conversation between Joanie and me. Joanie suffered from epilepsy. I was sincerely afraid that the stress of a large society wedding like her mother wanted, would not be good for her, and would moreover, create the perfect trigger for a seizure. The thought that this would happen to Joanie on what was meant to be the happiest day of her young life, was more than I could bear, and Joanie was worried as well.

Helen and Jerry Vinson were known for their extensive vacations and cruises. They would be gone for five to six weeks at a time and return home with stories about far away exotic places. The vacation in the spring of 1950 was to be an extended stay, which fit well into our plan. Joanie and I decided we would get married while Helen and Jerry Vinson were away, and not tell anybody about it. We had given it a lot of thought and done our homework to figure out where we could go to get married without raising suspicion among friends in Wichita Falls.

In small towns, the Courthouse is the center of all-important business. People would come from all over to get titles for their property, research information from births to deaths, buy up farm or oil equipment at bankruptcy auctions, and transact every manner of business. We knew that when we went to the court house to get our marriage license, it was only a matter of time before news of our visit would spread like wildfire through the community. Once this first step was taken, our timing would kick in, and there was no turning back.

When we arrived at the Wichita Falls Courthouse, we wasted no time in locating the office where marriage licenses were issued. The clerk met us with a faint smile. A young couple in a hurry to get in and get out was a familiar occurrence. Then, with hardly a glance in our direction, the clerk dropped a bombshell. She said each of us would need a shot to make sure our systems were clear of disease before a license could be issued. I had never heard this was a prerequisite to issuing a marriage license. This news ignited an immediate flashback in my mind of Leslie begging for mercy, as the emergency-room nurse approached him in the hospital with a shot of pain medicine for his crushed foot. Leslie was sure that would be the end of life as he knew it. The thought of witnessing the loss of my good friend that night in the ER was too much. The news a shot was required to get a marriage license was a deal killer for me. I was so scared at the thought of a shot, that I was ready to back out of the whole thing. I wasn't sure I could go through with the marriage under such risky circumstances. Pacing back and forth, wiping sweat beads from my face, while vehemently declaring my objection to taking a shot, alarmed Joanie. She had no idea what was going on with me. She patiently talked me down off the ceiling, and eventually I took the shot like a man, with a determined woman standing beside me.

Joanie and her Mother dreamed of a big wedding that would be the headliner social event of the year in Wichita Falls. Helen Vinson could imagine Jerry escorting Joanie, in her extravagantly trained wedding dress, down the long, extended aisle to give her away. I was not the son-in-law she hoped to see waiting at the altar. Clearly our plan to elope removed every possibility of the posh wedding Helen Vinson had in mind for Joanie. Nevertheless, the excitement that Joanie and I felt, skipping town to tie the knot, held its own romantic fascination.

Bob and Joanie Miller

Today, venue weddings are quite popular, and there is an abundant supply of wedding chapels and event spaces where couples can go to get married, surrounded by friends and family. This was not the case in 1950. A couple would typically get married at home, in a church, or before a Justice of the Peace (a judicial officer of a lower or court, empowered to preside over marriages and more). Neither Joanie nor I wanted to be married in a cold, sterile civil ceremony by a Justice of the Peace. We wanted to stand before a preacher to exchange our vows and be pronounced as man and wife.

We drove from Wichita Falls to Vernon, Texas, about 50 miles, and then 10 miles farther to Cromwell, Texas in my 1950 Ford. We didn't want to go as far as Oklahoma, so Cromwell seemed like a safe, secluded place for our secret marriage. Joanie and I were very nervous and talked about the "what if's" along the way. We hoped we could pull the wedding off without getting stopped by some well-intentioned friend of the Vinson's. I don't remember all the details, but Joanie was a better planner than I. She anticipated needing a change of clothing, as would any well-prepared bride. To plan for that, Joanie wore some borrowed pants under her dress, perfect attire for our get-away, once the ceremony was over.

With no GPS or cell phone in my 1950 Ford, we rolled into Vernon, Texas to look in a telephone directory for the name of a preacher in Cromwell. We had identified the place we would be married but not the preacher. To add to our paranoia, several older men were standing around on the corner of the street where we parked, watching our every move.

After all, we were two strangers in town, where even a new dog would be the topic of conversation for weeks on end. Joanie and I hurriedly crossed the street and headed for the nearest telephone booth beside the drug store. Thankfully, there was a directory and we found the name of a preacher in Cromwell and called ahead to say we were on our way. Heading back across the street to our car, we stepped off the curb, and the pants Joanie was wearing under her dress fell down around her ankles. The men on the corner saw the whole thing and were as shocked as Joanie. Imagine the embarrassment! Joanie could hardly speak as she and I grabbed the pants to free her ankles to walk, and we hurried back to the car.

Joanie wanted one of her friends to stand with her as a witness at the ceremony. I thought that would be risky, since our wedding was to be a secret, though I could understand Joanie wanting her friend along. We all met at the church in Cromwell in disbelief that we had gotten this far without being stopped. The preacher performed the ceremony, and we exchanged vows. Without fanfare, we left Cromwell for the drive back to Wichita Falls. Joanie and I couldn't believe we were Mr. and Mrs. The ride back was a sweet time of talking about the future and anticipating how Helen and Jerry Vinson would respond when they got the news that Joanie was married, and they had me for a son-in-law. We spent our first night in an apartment, but we knew our wedding bliss would be short lived. Joanie and I planned to go our separate ways to keep up the charade. She would stay at home with her parents after they returned from vacation, and I would stay at the college farm where I worked. I was headed into my senior year to finish my degree. Like most young couples, we wanted to spend all of our free time together, but our secret made that impossible.

As far as Helen and Jerry knew, or my Mom for that matter, our courtship was still blossoming. I would go by every day and pick up Joanie for a "date" and return her home at the appointed curfew. It was not ideal by any measure, but it kept peace with the family for the moment. It wasn't long after the wedding that Joanie's friend, who stood with her at the ceremony, told her boyfriend that Joanie and I were secretly married. Evidently, the boyfriend was trying to make some points to be considered for a job with Jerry Vinson, so he squealed on us.

Once Jerry got the news, he went straight to Joanie and asked outright if she and I had run off to Oklahoma and gotten married. Joanie denied the whole thing, pointing out that she was living there at home. (Besides, we didn't go to Oklahoma, it was Cromwell, Texas.) That held her Dad at bay for a short while, until he asked her again. Joanie broke down and started crying, admitting she and I were married while they were on vacation. Jerry immediately went upstairs to share the news with Joanie's mother. Helen nearly had a nervous collapse. She stayed in her room and cried for a week before she even came downstairs to talk with Joanie.

Joanie knew I would be in class, so she drove out to the college to give me a heads up that Helen and Jerry knew our secret. Joanie stood anxiously outside the class door whispering, "Daddy knows." My first thought was "Oh my God, how are we going to handle this? What is going to happen now?" I had to step up, and I thought "Look Miller, if you could handle the shot that was required to get the marriage license, you can handle this!"

I went immediately to my Mom's house to share the news with her. The telephone rang and it was Jerry Vinson wanting to talk with me. He said, "I understand you and Joanie got married while her mother and I were on vacation. I'm going to have an article in the newspaper, and I want to know your full name." For all I knew, he was preparing an obituary and wanted to make sure all the neighbors and friends knew I was the dead man. Thankfully, it turned out to be a wedding announcement. With that gesture, Jerry and I buried the hatchet. That was not the case with Helen. It took weeks before she'd say a civil word to me. It was very uncomfortable for Helen to be around us, but Jerry's goodwill made it tolerable for Joanie and me.

Joanie completed her course work and graduated from high school. We got an apartment but stayed there only a few weeks before opportunity came knocking. One of the hired hands at the Vinson ranch quit, leaving the ranch just outside Wichita Falls, in Iowa Park, high and dry and in need of someone to manage it. Jerry Vinson knew I was majoring in animal husbandry and he asked us to live there so I could run cattle and manage the ranch. Joanie and I agreed to move out to the ranch. It wasn't much to look at except for a beautiful lake, Bali Hai, and the Tahiti style house with a thatched roof, which created a kind of resort mood. Over the years, it had become a get-away for the Vinson's and their friends.

We could run about 40 mother cows on that 900-acre ranch. There was a corral already built, which would come in handy when we wanted to load the cattle and take them to the market in Fort Worth. That was a big deal! Ranchers from all over unloaded their cattle in "Cowtown" as we called it. The railroad ran right through the middle and train car loads of cattle were off-loaded in the Fort Worth Stockyards. Cowtown was the Mecca for buying and selling livestock. The perimeter of the stockyards was dotted with packing houses and eager buyers. It was big business and though Fort Worth is a beautiful modern city today, it is still Cowtown to the locals.

Joanie and I lived on her Dad's ranch during my senior year. Running the ranch was extremely demanding work. Bobby, Joanie's younger brother, came to the ranch to help. He was a good worker, and I was glad to have him. There was always something to do from digging post holes, to mending or stringing fences and more. Geefer and Beefer, the two ranch dogs, were often close at hand staring at us judgmentally, until we shared our lunches with them. Bobby and I enjoyed being together, even though it seemed like everywhere we went, we brought back a load of hay.

Joanie, the girl who grew up in the country club with all conveniences and luxuries, was living in a small shotgun house with no air conditioning, in the middle of the summer. It was a two-bedroom house built on the highest point on the ranch, so any breeze that came by, served to cool the house with the windows open. But it was summer in Wichita Falls. Today it is the home of the Hotter' N Hell Hundred, one of the oldest and largest cycling events in the nation, during which more than 13,000 riders from across the globe come to the area for four days of grueling cycling in the Texas heat.

One day in the middle of Summer, I came home and saw

Joanie, pregnant with our first child, lying on the living room floor, fanning herself. When I saw her, I felt like the lowest thing in Texas, since I couldn't afford to buy her an air conditioner. As I walked back out to the car to return to work, I saw a rattlesnake curled up in a dangerous, hissing knot on our driveway. I ran back inside to grab a gun, and just as soon as I leveled the revolver on the snake, who should roar into the drive but Joanie's father! I was so embarrassed, I couldn't speak. I was standing there with a drawn gun, an

Michael Miller, Son

angry snake and Jerry Vinson's only daughter sweating on the floor, two steps inside my front door! Luckily, Jerry took pity on us when he saw his daughter fanning herself on the floor and he sent over a brand-new window unit air conditioner. Joanie finally broke down one day and told me she was very unhappy at the ranch and she wanted to live in town as soon as possible.

My Mom came out to the ranch to live with us temporarily, to help out around the house. She was a huge help and a great encouragement to Joanie during those days. Mom and Joanie got along well, and I was glad Joanie had

Michael and Bob Miller

someone with her. The hours were long, as I was preparing for graduation and out taking care of the ranch. To pass the time, Joanie and Mom would try out new recipes, cook, bake, take care of the house, and prepare for the baby's arrival. On September 8, 1951, our son Michael was born in Wichita Falls. Mom generously offered to move to the ranch and babysit for us.

Mom had been diagnosed with cervical cancer about a year before. That was an unanticipated shock. Her health began to fail rapidly. I believe she willed herself to live, so she could see her grandson, because she hardly lived a month after Mike was born.

Losing Mom was traumatic for me and I was so thankful she got to see her first grandchild. She was a wonderful Mother. Joanie helped me through the hardest time of my life, and filled that tough time of loss with the evidence of what I had to live for.

As graduation approached, Jerry Vinson and I came to the same conclusion: There weren't enough cattle to make a living on the ranch of 900 acres. We found and negotiated a three-year lease on 6000 acres in Oklahoma between Chickasha and Oklahoma City. I bought 100 springers-heifers, anticipating a spring delivery of calves to establish the herd. The prairie-like Oklahoma pastureland provided plenty for the cattle to eat, unlike the Texas terrain filled by Mesquite trees and very little grass.

The cattle may have found Oklahoma a paradise but, when we moved there, it was a harsh demanding existence. Ask anyone and they will tell you that Oklahoma is known for its incessant wind. Oklahoma's wind resources are the eighth best in the United States. Even then, windmills dotted the landscape like a desert Holland and played an important role in agriculture. They pumped the water needed for livestock and crops. One would think that was a perfect set-up, but then the wind stopped blowing at its usual velocity. It was an unexplained disaster. I spent day and night on a tractor, gunning the engine to turn the power take-off shaft that I'd spliced to the water pumps, which the windmills were supposed to power. I was out there night after night, using the tractor as a stationary engine, turning the windmills, just to pump enough water to keep the cattle alive. There is no way I could possibly keep this up for three years. Jerry and I notified the property owners that we were ending the lease after one year. We sold the cattle to pay the bank note and we moved to Abilene. Joanie was delighted to be leaving the ranch and moving to town.

Bob in his study

10

FROM RANCHER
TO ROUGHNECK

A bilene was a different world from what Joanie and I had experienced. There was more opportunity of every kind, including the possibility of a social life, which definitely did not exist on the ranch. Joanie was happy to tell me her dad had an interest in a drilling company in Abilene with a friend by the name of Gilchrist. Jerry had loaned Mr. Gilchrist money to go into the drilling business. He stayed busy until the United States started importing oil from Saudi Arabia. More on that later.

I went to work for the Gilchrist Drilling Company. Joanie and I bought our first house in Abilene. I didn't want to pay more for the house that I could earn in three years. At the time, I was making $600 a month, so I could be comfortable spending up to $18,000 on our first home. As I recall, we bought the house in Abilene for $17,000. It was recently constructed, a brand-new house, and Joanie was very happy with it. At last she had a home of her own, and one that she could decorate as she wished. This home was a significant improvement from the dusty ranch house threshold I carried Joanie over when we first married.

After our first child, Mike, was born, the doctors told Joanie she could not get pregnant again. We were fortunate she carried Mike full term, but it took a toll on her health. When Mike was five years old Joanie and I decided to expand our family by adopting a baby.

A friend of the Vinson's in Wichita Falls was an obstetrician. They asked him to keep an eye out for a potential adoption. It wasn't long before a call came, that a baby girl had been delivered in the General Hospital to an unwed mother who could not take care of her. I was out on a drilling rig when Joanie called to tell me we had a baby girl waiting for us in Wichita Falls. I immediately hurried home to get Joanie. I suspect our delight and anticipation was like that of Les and Alice as they made their drive from Wichita Falls to Fort Worth to get me many years earlier.

Anticipating that a call would come one day to pick up our new baby, Joanie had made advance arrangements with her friend in Abilene to take care of Mike, so we were not delayed in getting on the road. Joanie and I headed on the 153-mile trek to the General Hospital in Wichita Falls to get our baby girl. We did not know what to expect regarding the policy of the hospital and adoption procedures. We were excited beyond words, and we prayed there would be no problems. To our surprise, the adoption procedure turned out to be uncomplicated. It resulted in the birth mother getting what she wanted, a good home for her daughter, and we got the grand prize, a beautiful baby girl for the price of the hospital bill. The certificate said the baby girl was born on January 31, 1956. We named her Marcia. We hurried home to Abilene to show Mike his new baby sister.

Marcia Miller, Daughter

In 1957, I was promoted at the Gilchrist Drilling Company, I'm sure with the help of Jerry Vinson. I was no longer a roughneck, but a contact man. I knew enough about the drilling business by that time, or so I thought, to carry this responsibility successfully. The drilling business was no different than any other successful business in that developing a customer base and delivering on our promise to drill the hole on time and at the best price, led to customer referrals, and referrals built the business.

As the contact man, my job was to make personal visits on potential oil and gas customers to secure the deal for Gilchrist Drilling Company to drill their wells. As I would close the deals with customers, our drilling crew moved our huge rigs and operations from place to place to drill. Back in those days, I was much too shy of a man for this line of work. I have always been a quiet person, but when I was in my 20's, that characteristic was very acute. I remember driving almost 150 miles one day to get a client to sign a document. When I arrived at his office, the secretary said the man had gone home for the day. I was too shy to make a fuss about the long drive I had made to get the signature, and so I said, "Thanks very much ma'am" and turned around, walked out the door and drove back home. Today, I find it hard to believe I did that, but it was very much in character for me at that time in my life.

Bob Gilchrist, my boss, decided that it would be a wise move for him to turn back two of his rigs, which were not needed at the time. When not in use, these rigs were a drag on the bottom line of the company's finances and could quickly eat up profit. Bob decided it would be a smart move to downsize by two rigs. That was a wise move.

Much to my surprise, Bob Gilchrist suggested that I take one of the rigs and go into the drilling business myself. I was intrigued by the idea and had secretly hoped one day I could do just that. The fact that Mr. Gilchrist thought I could be successful in the oil business as an owner, was a high compliment, and one I intended to justify. Never underestimate the power of encouragement, which you can extend to another person, and to seek opportunities to do that. Had it not been for Mr. Gilchrist's suggestion, who knows how long it would've taken me to start my own company.

There was only one problem, and it was formidable. I had no money to buy the rig or take up payments on it. With a wife and two small children, a roughneck's salary didn't leave much chance of accruing enough capital for a purchase like this.

I have always considered myself to be something of a horse trader. My negotiation skills had been well honed in high school from buying and selling cars. I believed if I could swing the deal, it would be the best possible opportunity for my family and me. Money was a problem, but it was not over yet. There was only one thing to do. I had to take my conviction and experience and parlay it into collateral. I mustered up my nerve to contact the people who owned the rig that Bob Gilchrist intended to return. They welcomed me and were curious to hear what I had to say. I laid all my cards on the table. "I don't have any money," I said, "to buy your rig, but I think I can keep it busy. If I can do what I say I can do, making the payments on the rig will not be a problem. If I can't do what I say I can do, then you get your rig back. It's a win-win for you either way." As I suspected, the last thing they wanted was a drilling rig sitting dormant, as a reminder of an investment that didn't work. They were in the equipment business to make money, not to accumulate a graveyard of unused equipment. We made the deal and it was official—The Miller Drilling Company was born. I was pumped!

At that time, there were no electronic databases, where potential customers could go to search for drilling companies. There was, however, a printed phone directory with a yellow pages section for businesses. This meant anyone searching for a drilling company could now find us, Miller Drilling. Now, when I called on customers, I had a whole new perspective. I was not there to get business for my employer. I was talking to customers to secure business for Miller Drilling Company! I was ready, able and eager to swim with the sharks and make my mark.

Reality soon set in when my potential customers, well-seasoned oil men, could not see beyond my youth. To them, I was just another kid who did not know the oil business. Granted I had a lot to learn, but experience had proven to be the best teacher. Nevertheless, the old-timers would say, "Well kid, you want us to do business with you? You're too young to know which end of the derrick goes up in the air!" They would often have a big laugh at my expense. To be successful in the oil industry, I had to prove myself and I had to get business. The only way I could land the drilling deal was to be the lowest bidder. Maybe then, customers would be willing to give me a chance.

Since the market I was trying to break into demanded that

I bid by the foot, I had to comply if I wanted the business. Bidding a well by the foot meant that I had to be very careful to calculate the exact number of days it would take to drill the well. Fortunately, I became quite good at my calculations and research. The geological studies we collected were my best friends. I poured over the studies, anticipating the degree of drilling difficulty, and I paid attention to all the details.

When I started working in the oil field, I was surprised by the waste. For example, some drillers would leave materials at the drilling site that could be reclaimed and used again. My days on the ranch prepared me well to run a frugal drilling operation. Looking back over my life, each opportunity, experience and challenge prepared me for the next.

As the lowest bidder, there was a huge risk. I must figure the job by the foot and get it right the first time. My customers were expecting one price for the whole job, regardless of the potential hazards it may hold for Miller Drilling Company. There were many variables, and many things that could go wrong and drive up the cost. I could have all the drilling experience I needed, but if I could not get the well down to the total depth needed to reach the oil, due to impenetrable obstacles, I got nothing. It was a winner take all situation.

Walking into the customer's door, I had to know everything about the rig from top to bottom. That allowed me to identify areas of waste. Eliminating the waste controlled my bottom line profit. I literally lived on the rig when I got a drilling contract and no one else would do that! Being ever present with the rig and crew allowed me to make sure there was no careless waste. I was focused and relentless, and I knew everything there was to know about the well and the ability of my crew. I had already figured out the number of days it would take to drill the well and how many bits would be needed, based on my geological research and exhaustive calculations. Some days there were fewer problems than others, and those days allowed me to drill faster than my calculations predicted. Thank God for the days which were free of obstacles, because they helped average out the more difficult ones.

I felt the weight of supporting my own family and paying the salaries of my crew, whose families were equally dependent on them. I wasn't even taking a consistent salary. Whatever I managed to make after paying my crew, buying material, and repairing rigs became my salary. There was one well that was my career turning point. It was a 4,000 foot well that I figured I could drill in 16 days. If I could drill the well in 16 days, I could gross $16,000. Grossing $1,000 a day meant I could make a profit. If I exceeded that drilling time, there was no profit.

At the time I bid on the well, I had one old Chevrolet truck that I had bought used. I spotted the truck at an auction and could get it cheap. This 27-year-old Chevy truck was our primary vehicle for relocating the rig once the well was finished. It had a winch on it and a single axle float. Most of the work trucks going down the highway today have tandem axles, but not this one. It was a flatbed, ready for work. We could pile our equipment on top of the flatbed and head out. If you saw it going down the highway today, it would surely get your attention. It was tired and well-worn from the heavy loads it carried for years, long before I got it.

It took approximately one week to move all the small trappings that I could haul with the Chevy. Then, the contract heavy trucks with large tandem floats moved the derrick and remaining equipment. Whether 20 miles or 100 miles to the next drilling site; a move was a move, and always resulted in downtime. On this particular day, it was a 20-mile move, and I had to get the equipment there and set up, anticipating the start of drilling the same day. My best plan failed when my crew, out of Abilene, approximately 100 miles away, showed up shorthanded. With all the equipment in place and the derrick set on the floor, I cut my losses for that day and sent my drillers back home, asking them to come back the next day with a full crew.

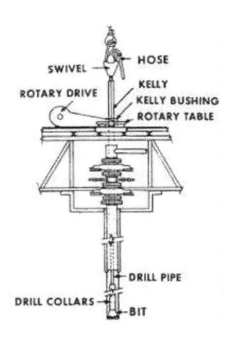

The crew arrived, and we started drilling the rat hole off the side of the rig for the Kelly. The Kelly is a rod attached to the top of the drill column in rotary drilling. It passes through the rotary table and is turned by it, but the Kelly is free to slide down through it as the borehole deepens. We also call it the drill stem.

Usually, drilling the rat hole was no problem. An hour after I started the process, we hit solid rock at 15 feet. When that happened, the drill bit was just jumping up and down against the surface of the rock. The drill bit was no match for the rock, and it was not budging. I had to figure out how to add weight on the drill bit if the well was to be a drilling success. The only thing of significant weight nearby, was my old, faithful, red Chevy truck. I concluded that if I backed up the Chevy truck and put a snatch block on the back of the truck, I could use it as a weight lever to exact the force I needed on the drill bit. I ran the winch line through the snatch block and tied it to the top of the swivel to lift the truck. I succeeded in getting enough of the truck's weight on the shaft to get the drill bit through the rock. It was an unconventional solution, but it worked. I can only imagine what a passerby who knew anything at all about drilling, thought at the site of that beat-up red Chevy truck dangling in the air.

Even though the Chevy worked well enough to force the drill bit into the rock, there were other problems. We had to keep a steady flow of drill mud going through the holes in the drill head. This is the single most important thing on a rig. Drill mud is pumped down through the shaft and, as it circulates back out the hole, it carries with it pieces of the rock that had been shattered by the force of the drilling process. This is called circulation, and circulation is one thing a driller never wants to lose. If circulation is lost, the drill bit will get bound up in chips of rock and lock itself hundreds of feet underground. When that happens, there is very little you can do. You can't just yank it out. The drill shaft may be

Oil Drilling Rig

hundreds or even thousands of feet long, and it rotates the drill head well enough, but, if you try yanking on it, it's going to stretch and snap like a wet noodle. The worst thing that can happen on a rig is to lose your bit down the hole. There is very little you can do but abandon your very expensive hole in the ground, with your very expensive drill bit stuck down it, and move on to drill another hole.

Soon after the Chevy helped us get the drill bit through the rock, we lost circulation, and I felt my bit lock itself at the bottom of a two hundred foot hole. I can't lose this bit, I just can't, I thought, I couldn't afford to drill another hole and even if I could move my rig, there would be nothing on the end of my shaft to drill with, I needed that bit!

When you ask most people what they think when they think of drilling for oil, the word that sums it up for them is 'roughneck.' It seems like a dirty business for men with broad shoulders. Words like 'tact' and 'delicacy' seem incompatible with 'crude oil.' But let me tell you, when you have a stuck drill bit that you absolutely can't afford to lose down a hole, the roughest operator will find himself with a surgeon's hands, because that is what it takes to unbind a drill head that is two hundred feet below. I slowly twisted the drill shaft, hoping to feel movement on the other end where the bit was bound up. It was agonizing to operate this huge machinery so delicately. As you can imagine, none of this equipment had been built for finesse. These machines were made to chew though rock at a fast speed. And to use it like tweezers took tremendous concentration.

Finally, I put enough tension on the shaft to back the bit up a few feet. The tension was very close to the breaking point on the shaft. I was able to inject enough mud down the hole to stir up the chips of stone at its deepest end. At the surface, the first sign I saw that this was not going to be a catastrophe, was the thickest foamy mud I had ever seen pouring from the drill head, loaded with chips. It looked less like a fluid than it did clay under pressure. It was close, but I got my drill bit back.

Bob on a cruise

11

THREE MIRACLES

I was a young man at the time I was drilling wells, but there is nothing that takes more out of a person than round-the-clock manual labor drilling for oil. Add to that, the mental stress of an impending disaster and the focus it took to unbind that drill bit, and I was one tired man at the end of that episode. I made my way to my car, got in the front seat and fell asleep sitting up. No sooner than I dozed off, my driller knocked on the roof of the car to wake me up. He said, "Bob, there's something wrong with the back engine."

Engines are the heart of the drilling operation. They turn the shaft sending the drill bit through earth and rocks to drill the well. I had two 225 horsepower LRO Waukeshas. Compounded together, my drill shaft had 450 horsepower behind it. That may sound like overkill, but applying enough power to a drill bit that was hundreds of feet long was no easy task. It was taxing on the engines. When we took the side panel off the back engine, the crankshaft was completely broken. There was not a thing that could have repaired that engine on site. I could do nothing about it. Like that broken engine, I was spent, and as tired as I've ever been. Shaken from my sleep, only to discover that I was about to be out of business, was a cruel nightmare. I stumbled to my car and sat in the passenger seat. It was still the middle of the night. I stared at my rig through the windshield. Words fail to adequately describe the depression that swept over me. I had worked myself like a rented mule for four solid years and yet, I was poorer than when I started.

The rig and all its problems faded, as my eyes drifted out of focus, staring into space. Time had stopped for me. I suspect my crew was also feeling the sting of another setback. While sitting in the dark, my eyes wandered to the door of my car's glove compartment. Without thinking, I popped the latch and it fell open. There, I saw my little New Testament Bible lying in the glove box. I reached for it and slipped it into my shirt pocket. Maybe it would bring me some kind of comfort.

I got out of the car, walked up the knoll, and from the top I had a full view of my drilling rig. I sat on a rock and looked down at my rig. Had it not been for the disastrous problems, it would have been a beautiful scene, with the bright lights that lit up the rig. But then I saw my drilling crew and all my men, forced to do nothing. It was a silent, eerie scene instead. Before I knew it, I was pouring out my heart and soul to the Lord. I felt such confusion. Up to this point, I had been fairly certain that God wanted me in the drilling business. I told God that was my understanding, sitting there on the rock. I asked God why I had worked hard for four years only to find myself farther behind than when I started. I asked God how I was ever going to meet my schedule with only one engine to turn the shaft. I asked all the questions that summed up my fears, but I didn't get instant answers.

My crews and their families were depending on me. Joanie, Mike and Marcia were also looking to me as their provider. The responsibility felt like a heavy weight on my shoulders. If I couldn't finish this well, I would not have enough money to pay my crews. My plea ended with, "God, if you want me to stay in the drilling business, then please, show me that is your will, in a way I can understand." I just wasn't getting it on my own and I needed confirmation. Considering all the problems and the fatigue I felt, I was about ready to throw in the towel.

MIRACLE ONE

About the time the horizon began to light up, I'd had finished pouring out my heart. I just sat there, quietly watching the sunrise. Instinctively, I reached in my shirt pocket and pulled out my little New Testament, without thought of where it might fall open. It opened to the fifth chapter of Romans. I didn't recall ever reading that Scripture before. I read down to the third verse where it says "Rejoice in your suffering knowing that suffering produces endurance, endurance produces character, character produces hope, and hope will not disappoint us for God's love has been poured into your heart through the Holy Spirit that has been given to you."

I read that Scripture over once more, and then I read it again, and a fourth time. Suddenly, I experienced the first miracle, a revelation. I thought that maybe I should just ask the Lord for help, instead of only despairing in front of Him. As I thought about that, it dawned on me that I had been trying to handle my career and these problems all by myself. It had been four years since I thought I had understood what the Lord wanted me to do with my life, and that was to drill wells. So off I ran to do it, thinking I would heroically succeed. But I realized that I only had the Lord's permission, but not His help, because I had been too proud to ask for that. Now I was asking for help, and it felt like a load had been lifted. I wasn't a lone-ranger any more. I knew beyond a shadow of a doubt that everything was going to be alright. Nothing had changed, and that crankshaft was still as broken as ever, but I knew it would be alright, now that I was asking God for help — real help!

I bounded off that knoll and flew up the stairs to the floor of my rig. I told my driller to keep it up with the one good engine because I was going to Abilene to see about getting another engine to replace the broken one.

MIRACLE TWO

The trip to Abilene was not as grueling as it would have been, had I not received that revelation. I walked into the Waukesha-Pearce office and announced I had broken the crankshaft on my back engine. They said, "We'll sell you a new one for $10,000." I immediately told them I didn't have $10,000. Unknown to me, the manager's office door was open as I talked to the salesman. He overheard our conversation, came out of his office and said, "What'd you say you needed?" And when I told him, he said, "Yesterday about five o'clock, our Wichita Falls store called me and said they had taken in an unusually good LRO on a trade and they wanted to know if I knew anybody that needed one?"

"What could you trade with me for it?" I asked.

He said, "If it's just a broken crankshaft on your engine, I could trade with you for $2,000."

"I'll take it," I said. "Call Wichita Falls and tell them to load the engine on the truck, and I'll call you for delivery when I've got my surface set."

I did not have $2,000, but my credit was good with the office and I knew there would be a bonus if we finished drilling ahead of schedule. That was my second miracle — to get an engine at any price, let alone at a cost which I could afford! This meant I could continue drilling, hoping for enough profit to pay my crew and pay off the engine.

MIRACLE THREE

I got in my car and headed back to the rig. There I would experience the third miracle. When I arrived back at the drilling site, the crew was already circulating drilling mud. They had gotten the hole made and the surface set. Instantly, I called Wichita Falls and said, "Head this way with that engine, I'm ready for you." Once the new engine was installed and the old one carted off, we finished that well in 14 days, a full two days ahead of schedule. Each day paid a $1,000 bonus, and that was the way I paid for a new engine without money, but with the Lord's help.

This was the turning point in my life and career. Those three miracles — hearing God tell me what to do through reading Romans in my New Testament, finding and getting the engine in Abilene I needed to finish the well, and finishing the well two days ahead of schedule, which allowed me to turn a profit — these were the distinctive three miracles that set me on the road to success. I finished the well ahead of schedule when it seemed hopeless to keep drilling. Make no mistake about it, from that point on I clearly knew and understood the source of my help.

In the months that followed I began to develop a reputation around Abilene as a reliable driller, and Miller Drilling Company began to grow. We plugged away, job after job, always doing our work better than anyone else and keeping our prices less expensive than others. In a market like the one we were experiencing at the time in West Central Texas, a market more ferociously competitive than just about any other, I knew drilling faster and cheaper than anybody else was the only way to get ahead.

Surprisingly, in 1961 I got a call from a person I had attended high school with named Steve Goss. Steve was a true wheeler-dealer back in school. He knew how to make things happen. He had purchased an option on 300,000 acres in the Arkoma Basin and needed a drilling contractor. Joanie knew, despite my growing reputation as an efficient operator, that we were still living hand to mouth in Texas. She was feeling the strain of trying to make ends meet and she was ready for me to try something else. So was I. With this opportunity, we packed up and moved to Arkansas.

Steve made an advance and a separate loan to cover

payroll, which helped me move my rig across Texas and set up business in Arkansas. Fortunately, the Arkansas job was day work. This meant that I was paid by the day, rather than by the completed wells. Not only did this mean I could pay down Steve's gracious loan more quickly, it also made it possible for me to buy a new house for my family in Fort Smith, Arkansas.

Geologically, Arkansas is very different from Texas. Arkansas is known as a natural gas state. The state has some oil down south, near Louisiana, but in the northern part, where Fort Smith is located, it is all gas. This ended up being quite fortunate for me.

It was much easier to drill for natural gas than for crude oil. With oil operations, there are the problems of circulating mud in the shaft, lining the shaft with concrete to protect the water table from contamination, and as I found out, keeping the engines going, to name a few.

Natural gas wells, however, can be drilled with compressed air. This doesn't require drilling mud, and compressed air drilling frees the rig up from complicated reservoirs and pumping equipment. All of this meant I was able to bring in gas wells faster than just about anybody in Arkansas. Not only did I use compressed air drilling, but I resided in the state, and Miller drilling Company was local. That gave me a competitive edge. I could be on the drilling site faster than any Texas firm could send rigs across the State line.

As I transitioned to a gas-only drilling operation, I began to build a reputation in Arkansas as the fastest and least expensive owner-operator around. This is what customers were seeking, trustworthy performance at the best price. My reputation was one thing, but I was limited in the number of wells I could drill with only one rig. It was at that moment of realization that another blessing fell on me.

I saw in the newspaper there would be a public auction on a drilling rig in Boonville. The sale was to be held on the courthouse steps in Boonville, about 30 miles southeast of Fort Smith. The newspaper indicated the rig was being kept there until the sale started. I wasted no time in getting to Boonville. I wanted to see and assess the rig for myself before the public auction began. I surveyed the equipment closely and wrote down every piece of the rig on my yellow pad. Beside each piece of equipment, I posted the amount that I could pay for each item. I knew equipment, and I was able to come up with a rough estimate, just by looking at the rig. The rig's worth was one thing, but what I could afford to pay was another. I knew my budget was considerably less than the rig was worth. By figuring closely, I came up with $15,000 as my top price— $15,000 in 1961 dollars was a huge amount, equivalent to more than $126,000 today.

After I made my estimates of the maximum I could pay, I headed over to the courthouse steps to wait for the auction to begin. When I arrived, there stood two men I knew. One was a direct competitor and the other was a used drilling equipment dealer from Odessa, Texas, from whom I had bought miscellaneous parts over the years.

The County Clerk came out the front door of the courthouse and announced in a loud voice that he was about to hold an auction to sell a drilling rig. That's what he was at the courthouse to do, he said emphatically, and he was going to do it! Though this was not a brand-new rig, I knew it was worth a great deal more than I was able to pay. The price of a new rig at that time would have been approximately $100,000, and today, it would cost close to a million dollars. My $15,000 top-dollar estimate was all I had to work with, and like the County Clerk, I was focused on my task; I intended to buy that rig!

The County Clerk asked the crowd gathered at the courthouse steps "What is my bid for the drilling rig?" The junk dealer from Odessa said he would give $100 for the rig. My competitor said he would give $200, and that's how the bidding started. Back and forth they went, upping the bid in $100 increments. I sat back quietly and let them bid each other up until the price had reached $3,000. Then, I spoke for the first time, raising the price by $1,000. The junkman raised my bid by $100 and my competitor raised his bid another $100, bringing the total bid to $4,200 for the rig. At that point I said, "I'll give $5,000 for it." The junk dealer let out a yelp, and said, "I'm not going to pay that kind of money for this rig. Besides, I would have to truck the thing back to Odessa. I'm out of here boys."

At this point my competitor and I were the only two left standing, to bid on the rig. He turned to the auctioneer and said he would give $5,100 for the rig, and I raised the bid to $6,000. He looked at me and angrily said," Bob, what on Earth is the matter with you? Don't you know how this works?" I said, "I came to Boonville to buy this rig. Now, feel free to go as high as you want. No more joking around." My competitor exclaimed, "Well if that's the way you're going to do this, Bob, that's it for me, I'm through." That was a remarkable experience.

Nothing is ever easy, least of all a bankruptcy sale, which is what drove this rig to the auction steps. When I went up into the courthouse to get the bill of sale for the rig, the judge met me and told me that he was setting the sale aside. I was shocked. The judge said the auction did not produce enough money to satisfy the debts the rig had been seized to pay. I said, "Judge, I was the high bidder. There were three bidders here." The judge said that he didn't care how many bidders there were. The auction didn't bring enough money, and he was going to stand by his decision to set aside the sale. I told the judge I was heading back to Fort Smith, but I would be back tomorrow with an attorney.

I headed home and called an attorney I knew from my church. I agreed to hire him for one day, starting the next morning. We lost no time in getting back Boonville the next day and headed straight to the courthouse and to the judge's office. My lawyer said, "Judge, my client tells me he was the high bidder on the auction held yesterday for the drilling rig. The auction was advertised in the paper. Three people showed up and in the legal auction that followed, my client was the high bidder among those present. Your Honor, this sale was legal from the start to finish, and I don't believe you can set the sale aside."

The judge was not impressed, and he was having none of my lawyer's logic. He said there was no way he would certify the sale of that rig at the price I had bid, which was the winning bid. After some bantering back and forth, the judge finally got sick of us, and he pointed to the Trustee of

Bankruptcy, also in the room. "This is the man whose job it is to make the ends meet between those who are owed and what the auction brought," said the judge. "Now the three of you go across the street, get coffee, and see if you can work it out."

Across the street we went, ready to talk. I was eager to hear what the Trustee of Bankruptcy had to say. I wanted to know what the problem was, since I had the winning bid for the rig in a legal auction. I also wanted his take on why the judge was not upholding the auction. Like the judge, the Trustee of Bankruptcy further emphasized that my bid was not even enough to pay the money owed to the crew. I asked how much was needed to do that and he said it would take $7,500. I thought for a moment and asked, "Are you telling me if I raise my bid to $7,500 you will give me the bill of sale for the rig? "He said, "Bob, that is exactly what I'm telling you." With that, I bought my second rig for $7,500 —half of what I had planned to pay, and at a 90% discount off of the new rig. This second rig made it possible for me to service Steve Goss' land options and keep my first rig in reserve for any new business I could stir up.

All through the 1960s, I made slow headway in the Arkansas drilling market. That era was difficult for owner-operators. We were at the mercy of oil prices impacted by the huge Middle Eastern oil fields coming online. Frankly, the unbelievable volume of their oil reserves, and ever-increasing efficiency of the ships transporting oil, meant that in order to compete, domestic production needed to be cheaper than ever–so compete I did, as efficiently as possible.

During this time drilling rigs were a dime a dozen, as local operators were driven out of business by foreign oil imports. I saw this as an opportunity to buy these rigs nobody else wanted. In my eyes, I saw a good deal and the chance to expand my capacity, but through the eyes of God, the future could be seen, including what was ahead.

In these lean years my rigs might spend months parked-up somewhere, waiting for a customer to call. A drilling rig is not like a tractor or truck. It is only good for one thing, and if nobody wants a hole drilled in the ground, it doesn't matter how many rigs you have; they are going to say parked in your lot like relics.

Most of the time when I would get a call for a job, the first word out of the caller's mouth would be, "How much do you charge, and do you have any room to come down on that price?". The potential customers would try to leverage the price down by reporting someone else had quoted a cheaper price and asked me to beat a competitor's price. While annoying, I knew that was indicative of the lean times. Everybody needed the absolute cheapest price possible in order to make the books balance. By the early 70s, I was doing well enough with my dozen rigs, but the market was by no means so rich, that expansion was a fore-drawn conclusion. But suddenly, everything changed.

12

THE WORLD COMES TO ARKANSAS

In 1973 the cartel that set production quotas for Middle Eastern oilfields, OPEC, decided to boycott the United States. The actual embargo only lasted for around six months, but it revealed how dependent our economy was on foreign oil. As the price per barrel climbed, it set off a mad scramble to ramp up domestic production. Suddenly, and seemingly overnight, the questions on the other end of my phone changed from "Can you work with me on that price?" After the embargo, every call and every caller started with the same inquiries: "We need a rig. Do you have one? How soon can you get it there?"

It was a gold rush on domestic production, and just as the '49ers learned, the ones who get rich during a gold rush are the people who sell the shovels. By the time the embargo ended, just six months later, the price on a barrel of oil had doubled, twice. Everybody in Arkansas was desperate to find something cheaper than overseas oil.

I was the owner-operator with the best reputation in the state. By 1976 I was doing well enough that I could do something I had never done before: I walked into an engineering firm and bought a brand-new rig, built to my own specifications. It was around this time I began to do something else I never thought I'd do. When people would call and say, "We need a rig, do you have one?" I actually began turning down work because I didn't have a rig for them. Mine were busy.

The domestic boom in Arkansas began to attract attention. A few years after the embargo ended, I got a call from the Tulsa World Newspaper. The Tulsa World was a very respectable newspaper, well known for their coverage of the drilling business. The first issue of the newspaper was published in 1905 and, today, it continues to be a trusted source of news. They wanted to know if I would be willing to talk to a reporter. I agreed at once. The reporter spent a day shadowing me, watching the ins and outs of running, what was by far, the most successful drilling business in Arkansas at the time. He drove back to Tulsa that night, and I spent the next week reading every page of the Tulsa World expecting to see the article, which the young reporter had prepared after our visit. Ten days later, I opened the newspaper and rather than the typical story I anticipated, I saw a full-page headline that read "The Chief of the Miller Drilling Company Said He'd Drill Anywhere, as Long as It Was in the Arkoma Basin." The whole page was taken up by the story the reporter had written. It covered my entire history in the drilling business, from the difficult, lean first years to the company's present dominance of the Arkansas market. It was essentially a full-page ad for Miller Drilling Company. As it turns out, I was not the only person reading the Tulsa World.

It wasn't long after that article appeared, I heard from a big New York conglomerate called W. R. Grace. This company was founded in the middle of the 1800s as a shipping firm and over time, the company had diversified considerably. Their main business interests were in manufacturing chemicals, and I suspect the chief in New York City, a man named Peter Grace, wondered why they were suddenly paying middlemen for their petroleum-derived feedstock. The short of it was this: Peter Grace decided to

move into drilling. It was an unknown area for expansion, and they needed someone with a successful track record to help them.

The company representative which Peter Grace sent to see me had clearly read the Tulsa World article. When W.R. Grace decided to get into the drilling business, he picked five of the largest basins for oil and gas in the United States and set about plans to buy the most successful drilling contractors in each of these basins. Grace's man called me and most of my competitors saying, "We'd like to come see you." I did not rush to schedule an appointment with him. He continued to call, and each time I expressed little interest in meeting. After several attempts to see me, one day in 1980, I agreed to meet him as a courtesy. I drove to the Fort Smith airport and briefly met with Grace's representative who was flying in on the company plane from Oklahoma City. In the course of our conversation, he said "I came over here to buy your company for W. R. Grace." And I said, "Well, what for?" He gave me a big figure. For a moment, I couldn't believe what I was hearing. I'd had no warning at all that he was prepared to make an offer.

The offer to sell my company was out of the blue. Instinctively, I replied, "My company is not for sale." Stunned, Grace's man thought a minute and said, "Do you mean you're going to turn down this offer?" I said, "Well, my company is not for sale." Without further conversation, he headed back to Oklahoma City.

While driving back home, I was thinking, why on earth would I want or need to sell my company? This business is a license to print money. I was making more money than I ever thought possible. As surprised as I was about the Grace offer, I must admit that offer was getting pretty close to the magic line of where a man starts to think about never having to work again. I remembered a quote by E. Stanley Jones in his book *Along the Indian Road,* which I found to be prophetic, "There are two ways to be rich - one in the abundance of your possessions and the other in the fewness of your wants".

About three weeks later, Grace's man contacted me again for another conversation. W. R. Grace had increased the offer for Miller Drilling Company, almost doubling it. My answer was still "No, I am not going to sell". The last thing the Grace company representative wanted to do was to take my second rejection back to Peter Grace.

Over the next several weeks, the thought of selling my company began to seep deeper into my mind. Subconsciously, there seemed to always be a prayer for wisdom about this issue in my mind. I talked to Joanie about Grace's offer to buy Miller Drilling and, like me, she was enjoying the success we were already experiencing. She knew how much I loved Miller Drilling Company, but she also knew the stress of running the operation.

I awoke early one morning, as though an alarm clock had gone off in my head. At that moment, right then and there, I had the distinct feeling in my mind and heart, that the timing was right for me to sell my company. The feeling was similar to the revelation I experienced in Miracle 1, many years earlier. It was like a nudge from God. During all those times the W. R. Grace Company continued to pursue buying my company, I honestly had no inkling that I would sell. It was the farthest thing from my mind. I realized that in my resistance to the thought of selling Miller Drilling Company, I had not so much as kept the business card Grace's man had given me. I had no idea how to contact him to let him know my decision. Oh well, I guess that's that.

As Providence would have it, Grace's man contacted me again shortly thereafter. This time I sensed a difference in how he was talking. The offer on the table had jumped again. At the end of the conversation, Grace's vice president said "Bob, you need to realize Peter Grace is not satisfied with no." I told Mr. Grace's representative that in order for me to seriously consider selling, I would first need to talk personally with Peter Grace. I had crucial questions for which I needed answers. Grace's vice president immediately invited Joanie and me to New York City so I could meet Mr. Grace.

From the first moment we arrived In New York City, until boarding our flight home, the trip was carefully designed to demonstrate to me what money could do. Joanie and I were treated like royalty. We were put in a penthouse on Fifth Avenue, overlooking the city, taken out to dinner and a Broadway show by the vice president of the company on Thursday evening, and again on Friday evening.

They knew I had been making money hand over fist in Arkansas, but it was clearly Grace's aim to show me what New York money looked like, and how to spend it. But despite this, it wasn't until I met Peter Grace, that I decided for sure to sell.

Early Saturday morning, mid-November 1979, the vice president took me to meet Mr. Grace. The lobby, elevators and offices were a ghost town that Saturday morning. There was no one around as we boarded the elevator. After brief introductions, the company vice president left the room, leaving Peter Grace and me alone to meet high-atop his skyscraper office.

Mr. Grace said, "Bob, I understand you're thinking about selling your company?" Despite my growing feeling that this might be the opportune moment to sell, my instincts die hard. As soon as I heard the words come out of Mr. Grace's mouth, all my imaginings, of what the money from the sale of my company could do in this world, flew out the panoramic windows lining Mr. Grace's office, and I immediately went into one-on-one salesman mode. I said, "Mr. Grace, I started that company when I was twenty-seven years old. There is no question about it, I have some of the finest crews in the oilfield, but I am concerned about what selling my company would do to them. In fact, I probably have the finest small, independently owned drilling company in the United States. I also have a son who is graduating from law school, and a son-in-law who works for me. Tell me Mr. Grace, given all of this, would you sell your company to W. R. Grace if you were me?"

As I reflect on that moment in Mr. Grace's office, part of me, to this day, still can't believe I talked to a man like Peter Grace that way. But the instinct for a hard sell doesn't care whether you're talking to a guy who is barely getting by, or to one of the richest men in the United States.

Peter Grace smiled at me when I asked him if he would sell the company if he were in my shoes. Then, his smile vanished and I saw his face and gaze become deadly serious. Peter Grace said, "Mr. Miller, yes I would sell. I would, for three reasons. Number one, I have seven children. Only one of them even works for this company, and he has no desire to run it. Number two, if we make our deal, your people will be my people, and I feel about my employees the same as you do about yours." Then, he made the third point, saying, "If we make our deal, it'll make your estate planning a whole lot simpler." By this last point, Peter Grace meant that the money to buy my company would be publicly traded, and I would know what it was worth on any given day. Furthermore, my estate would be subject to lower taxes when it came time to distribute it to my children. His last point got my attention.

I asked Mr. Grace for time to think about it, but as I left the office on the top floor of his palatial office building, I had already made up my mind to sell my company. W. R. Grace wanted me to stay on for five years after the sale, to help run the company. When I thought about the sack of money I'd walk away with after the sale, plus the fact I would still have a job for at least five years, I just didn't see any way I could lose. Besides, there were other things on my mind.

I was five days past my fiftieth birthday when the sale closed, and that still seems like youth to me now. I had grown to dread those frequent midnight phone calls I would receive about drilling problems. Nobody who runs his or her own business has ever gotten good news when the phone rings in the middle of the night. I am completely certain that the only reason I am alive today, is that the Lord allowed me to see how stress eats at a person, and how He led me to give all that up, before it had a chance to take its ultimate toll on me.

Joanie and I headed back to Fort Smith from New York. In the weeks that followed, the details of the sale were finalized.

Once the final price was worked out, and all appropriate agreements negotiated, I called Peter Grace to let him know I was going to sell my company to him. He was very gracious and glad to get the news.

I must say, it was a strange experience working at my company after I sold it. Four times a year the presidents of all the drilling companies that Grace had bought would meet to discuss operations. A Grace vice president was always in attendance. The job of my former competitors and me, was to do what this New York manager asked of us. Every quarter he would ask the same question: "How many more rigs can you rig up?"and every quarter we would weld more rigs together by cobbling pieces of used rigs from parts bought piecemeal, and we would also by new rigs out right to meet expectations.

This process of running our business with New York management and money, went on for about four years. Every year, the company asked for more rigs than the year before. We had amassed over 1000 drilling rigs. At that point, I started to get a feeling that even though the market in domestic drilling is using all this equipment, that level of demand in the marketplace could not be sustained. That's not the way the oil business works. In one of the quarterly meetings in 1984, I spoke up saying, "Look, we're up at about a thousand rigs. I think we ought to hold at that number and see what this drilling business is going to do." Grace's man did not even give me the courtesy of an answer. He did not want to hear or acknowledge my concern or suggestion. The nearest thing I got to a response was from his assistant who leaned over to me and whispered "Bob, you don't understand. W. R. Grace has never had a business that made this kind of money." We continued to acquire rigs at break-neck speed.

The oil business during boom-time coins money like few other ways of making a living. These New York men had gotten a taste from this fire-hose, and convinced themselves the flow would never stop. Every quarter we were asked to field more and more rigs. By 1985 W. R. Grace's unshakable belief in a bull oil market had pushed the total rig count we were running in the United States up to 4,400. It was an unbelievable number, and I knew it could never last. Unfortunately, I was right.

Before I left Grace, I saw that number of rigs plummet to 2,700. Hal, one of the company vice presidents came to see me. I picked him up from the Fort Smith airport and took him to his hotel. He said, "Bob, the rig count's down a little bit, isn't it?" I replied, "Yeah, it is." He asked, "Well, this thing is going to turn around isn't it?" I said, "Hal, I've seen it below a thousand." Hearing that, Hal got a stricken look on his face and said, "Oh, Bob don't tell me that." With that, he got in the company airplane, went back to New York City, took early retirement and moved to Florida.

13

GROWING
SPIRITUALLY

Around the time Joanie and I moved from our ranch in Oklahoma to Abilene, I had the first spiritual transformation of my life. The drilling contracting business was about as slow as it has ever been for me, with weeks going by without a phone call from anybody who needed to drill a well. I had been feeling what is described as "a calling." I had always been a church-going man, that is how I was raised. I chose Christ at the age of twelve, but around about 1955, I began to wonder if attending church was enough to satisfy me. Going to church once a week had begun to feel like a rote, weekly dose of medicine. In my heart, I felt strongly that God was more than a weekly experience, and that if I was serious, I should walk beside Him every moment of every day. Even though my parents took me to church, and as an adult we attended church, I don't recall there was much emphasis on a personal relationship with Jesus. We learned a lot about Jesus' life, and his way of seeing things, but little about personal interaction with him on a daily basis. Honestly, I was not sure what to do about my sense of needing more spiritually. All this changed when I first heard E. Stanley Jones preach.

Who was this man? Well, to the rest of the world he was Eli Stanley Jones and he lived from 1884 to 1973. He spent seventy years in the ministry of Jesus Christ. He was an evangelist, missionary, author of twenty-eight books, statesman, Bishop-elect twice (he resigned before consecration), founder of the Christian Ashrams, ecumenical leader, and spokesman for peace, racial brotherhood, social justice, and constant witness for Jesus Christ. Jones was a confidant of President Franklin D. Roosevelt. He was nominated twice for the Nobel Peace Prize, and his ministry in India brought him into close contact with that country's leaders including Jawaharlal Nehru, Rabindranath Tagore, and Mahatma Gandhi.

Jones had the idea that Jesus Christ was a universal figure, not just a Western figure. Christ had been wrapped up so much in Western culture that it's hard to get a handle on Him, in order to get that all-important personal relationship with God. Jones' method (initially used in India), which led to the creation of The Christian Ashram movement in the United States and globally, presented Christ as the universal Son of Man, stripped of the accumulations of Western culture, or any particular culture for that matter. This is how Brother Stanley put it in his writings:

> *When I first went to India to share Christianity, I was trying to hold a very long line – a line that stretched from Genesis to Revelation, on to Western Civilization and to the Western*

Christian Church. I found myself bobbing up and down that line fighting behind Moses and David and Jesus and Paul and Western Civilization. There was no well-defined issue. I had the ill-defined, but instinctive feeling that the heart of the matter was being left out. Then I saw that I could, and should, shorten my line, that I could take my stand at Christ and before that non-Christian world refuse to know anything save Jesus Christ. I saw that the gospel lies in the person of Jesus, that he himself is the Good News and that my one task was to live and to present him. My task was simplified. My task was not only simplified, it was vitalized. I found that when I was at the place of Jesus I was at every moment upon the vital.[1]

This is what began Jones' great adventure throughout India. He realized that he could simply describe what God had done in his life and could do in the lives of others as well. This insight turned Brother Stanley into the one of the great evangelists of the 20th Century. Using this insight, Jones began speaking constantly to ever growing audiences of educated non-Christians. He presented Christ as a disentangled Christ, the savior apart from the trappings of Christianity, apart from Western Civilization. He presented Christ as a savior for everyone, belonging to all cultures and all races and the answer to every last human need.

My friend Bob Tuttle, a professor of theology, called Jones *"the greatest missionary/evangelist of the last century, whose passion, humility, and total commitment to Jesus Christ and His Kingdom comprise a story that is forever relevant."[2]* That was Brother Stanley as I knew him.

---

1 Jones, *Christ of the Indian Road*, pp. 11-12.

2 Tuttle, *In Our Time: The Life and Ministry of E. Stanley Jones*, p. 13.

While Jones was in India, he came to know about the very old tradition of ashrams. These were spiritual retreats that men like Gandhi and Rabindranath Tagore had organized to restore the souls of weary people. Jones believed that the Christian faith was a universal one. Because of this he tried, as hard as he could, to translate the Christian faith into the local form of spirituality. The ashram became that form. The Christian Ashram for Jones meant Christian fellowship, in the context of Indian spirituality. For example, the Indian Ashram has a Guru, or Head, around whom the Ashram revolves and from whom it takes its characteristics. The Christian Ashram has a Guru, but it is not a human guru, rather it is Jesus Christ.

Jones was often asked this question: "What does it take to become a member of the Christian Ashram Group?" His answer was:

> *We have one qualification and only one. Do you want to be different? If you want to be different, come on. But if you don't want to be different, we can do nothing for you. The crux of being made different is found in self-surrender. Only when the self is surrendered can you cultivate your spiritual life around the new Center – Christ, and Christ in control. Then everything falls into its place.*[3]

Jones took what he had learned in India and brought the Christian Ashram to the United States in 1940. It was at one of these American Christian Ashrams in Abilene, Texas, that I first felt the power of a personal relationship with Jesus Christ.

---

3 Jones, *A Song of Ascents*, p. 231.

What was the Ashram like? The first meeting at an Ashram is called the "Open Heart." Participants are asked, "Why have you come? What do you want? What do you really need?" The questions are often so probing that to the surprise of many, people speak from the heart about their deepest needs, hurts and challenges. At the end of the Ashram, the "Overflowing Heart" is held, where participants discover what the Ashram fellowship and time with God has done for them. Problems and anxieties are dissolved away by the redemption you feel in this group experience. The changes you can undergo here are remarkable. The Open Heart and the Overflowing Heart are the two pillars of the Christian Ashram. Between them are several other opportunities for fellowship with the Holy Spirit, including a 24-hour prayer vigil, accompanied by small prayer groups where participants pray for each other. Each day begins with an hour of Devotions before breakfast, half spent in silence with your Bibles and half in sharing what you have found in it.

After breakfast, there is the Bible Hour, where you study holy writ and look for Jesus in it. Following the Bible Hour is the Church at Work Hour, where participants step out of the Bible into the world around them to see how they can function as Christians, contributing to the world. The afternoon is for fellowship and recreation. Before the evening meal there is a vesper service. After dinner, the Ashram day finishes with an evangelistic service during which the group is given a chance to affirm publicly the spiritual decisions made during the day. This was the time I first heard Brother Stanley preach.

The final session of the Christian Ashram is the

Overflowing Heart where the personal "transformations" are shared. Jones wrote:

> *The purpose of the Overflowing Heart is to do what one of the lepers did when, having been healed, turned back and fell at the feet of Jesus and said: 'Thank you, thank you.' It attaches the changed person to Jesus Christ and not to the Ashram movement.*[4]

But who was this man to me? Hearing Brother Stanley preach at that first Christian Ashram in 1955 changed my life. He showed me it was possible to walk alongside God in my daily life.

E. Stanley Jones was a remarkable man by anyone's definition, but to me, the most praiseworthy thing about him was his ability to make a personal relationship with Christ obvious to anybody who heard him preach. The feeling that I have been walking with God every moment of my life since, has been the greatest blessing.

As a steady Ashram-goer, I began to talk to Brother Stanley, just as I would my own preacher. He had the most amazing ability to make you feel relevant, as though you were the single most important person he could be talking to at that moment in time. Remember, I was a fairly retiring person at that point in my life, and rare were the moments when I thought I had the right to ask something of other people. With E. Stanley Jones, however, everything was different.

After I experienced the miracles on my drilling rig, when my crankshaft broke and I despaired of ever finishing the

---

4 Jones, *A Song of Ascents,* p. 226.

well on time, I began to feel more and more as though I ought
to be in the ministry. As I read those verses in Romans, sitting
on that knoll at the breaking of dawn, and throughout the
weeks that followed, this thought came back to me: "Bob, you
need to be out there, leading the people back to God, as
you've been led."

But what did I know about being a minister? Being a
steady church-going man and crossing the invisible line that
separates the flock from the shepherd is no small thing for an
ordinary layperson to contemplate. I felt absolutely caught
between two feelings: I dearly needed to minister to others
and share this good news I had been blessed to receive, and
obviously, I was a drilling contractor without great ability for
public speaking or theological training.

I went to Brother Stanley with my quandary. I
approached him at an Ashram and told him what had
happened to me. He listened attentively as I talked about the
three miracles I experienced, and how they made me feel
more certain than ever that I was supposed to have a ministry
of my own. Then I asked him if I should give up the drilling
business and become a preacher.

E. Stanley Jones looked at me and told me something that
completely changed my life. He said, "Bob, all God wants is
you, and if He has you, He will use you in whatever you
choose to do. The Lord needs businessmen just as much as He
needs preachers."When I heard that, it made perfect sense.
That insight gave me the greatest feeling I've ever felt in my
life. I had spent the hardest years of my youth pouring myself
in to the drilling business, and I had picked just about the
worst time in the market to start. America had an insatiable

appetite for oil in the 1950s and the market in Texas for getting it out of the ground was fiercely competitive. This was the place I had chosen to make my living, and by driving myself as hard as possible, I was just barely keeping my head above water. In the midst of all this toil and sweat and anxiety I found myself thinking of things beside success in the drilling business, thinking of God and what I owed my fellow men. I felt so torn, and then I found this man, E. Stanley Jones, who spoke to the spiritual side of me more profoundly than anyone else I'd ever met. He told me that all this toil and anxiety, and pride in my hard-won accomplishments was not what God wanted. God wanted me. Jones spoke a few sentences to me that day in 1955 which brought the two ends of my life together in union: my life's work and my heart's need to be nearer to God. Jones made me realize that I was good enough for God just the way I was. That realization is the kind of gift that only the most gifted, extraordinary teachers of God's word can convey, and it has been the single most precious thing, after life itself, that anyone has ever given me.

14

THE FIRST DAY OF
THE REST OF YOUR LIFE

It is not easy to say all the ways walking with Jesus Christ has made my life infinitely better, but the first thing it did was to give me that personal ministry I wanted. When you walk with Jesus and can feel Him walking beside you, everything becomes easier. Now I don't just mean that the hard things become easier, although they certainly do, but the biggest reward is how easy the simple things become.

I pray every day, not out of duty to God but out of gratitude. It has become second nature to me to let God know how grateful I am for my life, my family, this Earth and all the things in it. All are gifts from God. Some people have a terribly heavy idea of prayer. To some, praying is what you do when everything else you have tried under your own steam has failed to solve the problem. For me, prayer and walking with Jesus have made my appreciation for the blessings I have received natural, as natural as breathing. I find that prayers of thanksgiving weld up inside of me with almost every step I take and praying keeps me focused on the source of my strength. I am able to see the beauty of every little moment I live, even the practical ones. Flying is a good example.

I have always loved flying, ever since that day in the 1930s when the first airplane made its debut in Wichita Falls. I was hooked for life. I imagined what it would be like to be one of the people who had the price of a ticket to fly on the plane that day. I imagined looking out the plane windows high atop the trees and seeing a different, greater view. Selling my company gave me the ability to do many things. Money is a fine thing, but unless you use your imagination to understand the freedom it holds, it just sits there. My imagination took me to the skies.

Flying is different from anything else. Flying is what freedom feels like. Flying is freedom. Flying is one of the best feelings in the world to me. If someone asked me what a personal relationship with God is like, I would say it feels like breaking through a deck of low, obscure, bumpy clouds in your aircraft and seeing the clear, sunny, smooth sky above. Flying has been the most practical, yet useful thing in the world to me. I believe I would have seemingly been at odds with myself without it.

Back in the middle 1950s, when I was still working for another drilling contractor, I got my first taste of flight. The contractor I worked for hired a plane and a pilot to fly us to remote towns in order to call on two or three customers. The contractor nor I had ever flown in an airplane before. He liked it so well, he plunked down a retainer as soon as we got back to the airport to secure the plane for future use. We had twelve hours a month of flight time at our disposal, whether we used those hours or not.

Flying ignited my imagination too. I took the ground school course required to fly and began to take lessons with a flight instructor in my spare time. Pilots, especially in their first years, want to be up in the air as much as possible, to build up hours of flight time. Good pilots spend hundreds of hours in the air, experiencing all types of weather conditions throughout day. Learning to fly is easy, that's just classroom stuff, but becoming a good pilot is a slow, painstaking process, like mastering the piano. The logbook tracked our hours of retainer flight time used from month to month, and it let me know the unused hours still available. I kept a close eye on that logbook and when I saw we had some hours left at the end of a month, hours that could not roll over into the next month, I would take our plane up and just fly. This allowed me to fly the required solo hours for my pilot's license. Flying became an asset in my career as a drilling contractor and served me well. I flew my own plane for years.

The oil field is filled with stresses. I sold my business because I knew it would kill me, eventually. In the lean times before 1973, it was almost a monthly occurrence that I would have to tell someone I couldn't keep them on. I was called at all hours of the night to deal with crisis after crisis. It got to the point that I felt like was in a permanent crouched position, always ready to absorb some blow or spring into action to prevent a catastrophe from spiraling out of control. That is the oil field. Success is not just the product of hard work and God's grace. It requires total devotion of body and mind. When there was a snow day, I called up everyone who worked for me to ask if they needed a ride. If they couldn't drive, I would pick them up. It always seemed to me that in life you either care, or you don't. But this takes a toll.

It's not easy to explain how very much flying felt like the antidote to stress. Time after time, I would take off in my plane with low clouds above me, climb through the grey cloud cover and then burst out above them. Seeing the whole universe open in that moment of breaking through was like seeing God. I loved the drilling business and the challenge of working deep, deep in the earth, but there is no experience in the world like being up above the clouds and knowing how birds feel every time they fly.

Meeting E. Stanley Jones gave me a sense of ministry. I really believe that as I carried on my business as a drilling contractor in the Arkoma Basin, I was performing ministry. I did my best to care for those around me and help anyone I could. Even more, I was determined to be the best drilling contractor I could, because God wanted it that way. In the days and years after my experience at Brother Stanley's Ashram, I lived in unshakable faith that I was on the right path, and that God would use me for good. After I sold my company to Peter Grace it became clear what that good would be.

I closed my deal and sold my company on January 15, 1980. The very next month, during the dead of winter in February, I was lying in bed one night while a terrible winter storm raged outside. As I was lying there, I could hear the eerie sounds of bits of sleet tapping against the side of the house. When I heard that sound, I rolled out of bed and got on my knees to thank God that I had such a good, warm place to sleep at night. My very next thought after this prayer was a question: Well Bob, what about the people who don't have a warm place to sleep tonight? What about people who haven't any place to sleep at all? Where are they and what is this night like for them?

So, I asked the Lord, "Are you trying to tell me to start a mission? If you are, Lord, you're going to have to show me where you want it, and you're going to have to show me somebody to run it." My family often giggles when I tell this story, because it sounds like a bit of negotiation, but I just wanted and needed God's help – much like the revelation I had experienced with the first miracle.

Within a week, I was driving down 3rd Street in Fort Smith and I saw a For Sale sign outside the Westside Baptist Church. I went in and talked to the preacher, and I asked, "Why are you selling your church?"

The preacher said, "Well, it's not a good location for the church." I then asked what all goes with it and I learned the church building and the lot next to it were included.

The preacher gave me the selling price and I left saying I would get back in touch with him later. As I drove away, I was determined to buy that church. I said aloud, "Well, thank you, Lord, you've shown me where you want the mission. Now, please show me somebody to run it."

The very first person I asked was a man named Jon Grimm. Jon and I had served on a couple of boards together, and we shared a mutual concern for people in need, particularly the homeless. He had recently sold his company too. When I told him what I felt called to do, the first words out of his mouth were, "Bob, I would just love to run a mission with you." Two out of two, Lord, thank you! That was the beginning of Community Rescue Mission. We had a place, and Jon as its very capable first director. I suppose one could say Jon and I were "Mission Comrades."Jon Grimm and his wife Sam, were working for Frank Turner at the Van Buren Gospel Rescue Mission at the time. It was about to close and they were trying to keep it open.

I bought the church and, with Jon's help, it took us about a year to get everything up and running. By March of 1981, we

Hope Chapel at Community Rescue Mission

were full steam ahead, and that Mission filled up quicker than I ever thought possible. There were so many people to help in Fort Smith and before long, we were looking at the vacant lot beside the church for expansion. We decided to build a 12-room motel-type unit on the vacant lot, which we still use today for families. To keep up with demand, I bought a building across an alley that cut through the church property. We fixed it up and used it as a men's dormitory.

About eighteen months after we had bought the land and renovated this building, I was walking through that old building, and on that particular day, I saw it with fresh eyes. It looked so dingy and sad to me. I could never imagine wanting to sleep there, let alone live in that building. We

Bob inside the Hope Chapel at Community Rescue Mission

razed that thing and built a nice new building in its place.

The new structure included a big dining room and full kitchen to provide meals to our residents. By the time we had finished the new dormitory, it became clear why the congregation of the old church had been eager to sell. Nothing in the old church building had been built up to code. There was no foundation, only wooden piles driven into the earth. There was no drainage and every time it rained heavily, the water flowed like a river into the church. One night during a storm, lightning struck the old church and burned it to the ground. The only thing we salvaged was a huge wooden cross, and enough insurance money to build a new chapel. God provides!

We built a new chapel, up to code this time. I put the old cross on the wall of our beautiful, new chapel where it still hangs today. Shortly after we built that new chapel, I felt a need to add something to it, but I was not quite sure what it ought to be. After spending time thinking and praying about it, I decided to write a short text to express my hope for the people who prayed in our Hope Chapel. I had the text engraved on a wooden plaque and hung on the wall. I'll include it here because it's the nearest thing I have to a personal testimony of how seventy years of walking with Jesus makes you see things:

> *The most important decision we make in life is what we are going to do with Jesus. Do we acknowledge him as our Lord and Savior, or do we believe he was just a prophet? Let's look at the facts.*
>
> *In the beginning was the Word, the Word was with God, and the Word was God. The word became flesh and lived*

among us. Jesus said, 'I have come that you might have life and have it more abundantly.' God did not send His son into the world to condemn the world, but that the world through Him might be saved. Toward the end of his life on Earth, Jesus told the sister of a dead man named Lazarus, before He raised Lazarus from the dead: 'I am the resurrection and the life, if anyone believes in me, even though he dies yet shall he live, and he that lives and believes in me shall never die.' Then to show the world how much he loves us He allowed himself to be crucified, die, and be buried. Then, on the third day, He arose from the dead just as He said He would. Jesus wanted us to know what God was really like and to know that God loves us. If we ever doubt that, all we have to do is look at Jesus. When Jesus left the Earth, God poured His love into our hearts through the Holy Spirit that has been given us that we might continue to have His presence with us each day. God is as near as our next breath.

So, it is with the sure knowledge of these facts that this Hope Chapel is dedicated to the one who created us and loves us, and will continue to love us throughout eternity, and if we but choose, we can return the love God so freely gives.

My dearest hope is that this writing will make one thing clear to anyone who reads this plaque: if Lazarus could be dead and buried and yet still available to the salvation love of Jesus, how much better are your odds, still alive as you are?

Jon Grimm and his wife provided hands-on leadership for many years and contributed greatly to the Mission's success. After Jon died, Sam and their five children remained at the Mission for a time to continue the work. Throughout the last 37 years, the Community Rescue Mission has served more than 2,000,000 free meals to people in need. We have the capacity to sleep 50-75 people at a time. Today, our focus is on serving families and children who are homeless. We provide case management, life skill classes, job search assistance, wellness checks, safe shelter, food and clothing to help homeless families find their way to a healthy life, gainfully employed, and in a home of their own.

Several years ago, I bought a warehouse across the street well below market price, from a man who was ready to retire. It houses our clothing ministry. Many parents and children arrive at the Mission with all their belongings in a plastic shopping bag. Thanks to the generosity of First Lutheran Church, other congregations, and people in our community, we now have excellent seasonal clothing of all sizes.

In that same large building, we opened space for a Sack Lunch operation in association with St. John's Episcopal Church. This cooperative effort allows us to participate in serving thousands of free meals to hungry people a month.

Miller Branch Library, Fort Smith, AR

I have always had a good head for figuring costs. When I was trying with all my might to succeed in the fiercely competitive Texas drilling market, this was absolutely an essential skill. Drilling work was calculated by the foot in those days, and if you couldn't look at a site and see all the costs right away, then you were on the short path to going broke. I feel blessed to have carried this skill into my work with the Mission. I have tried my best to make every dollar stretch, so as to do the most good possible. Our budget at the Mission is totally funded by donations from our community. We are so thankful for the generosity of people who care, and share our commitment to serve others. We do as much good as possible, using every donated dollar wisely, as good stewards of all entrusted to us. We are blessed with an excellent group of men and women on our ecumenical board who represent supporting congregations throughout the Fort Smith area.

Thanks to the support of our community, this year, we will begin to fulfill our visionary master plan to renovate all the facilities at Community Rescue Mission to make an even more home-like setting for families and children.

A few years after we got Community Rescue Mission up and running, Joanie was the main force behind another project to help Fort Smith. She always loved books, and Joanie had gotten to know almost everyone who worked at the main downtown library. She told me that she and her friends at the central library were thinking of building several branch libraries around town to keep up with the demand for books throughout the community. Joanie and I were very happy to help build one of these branch libraries.

We were thrilled when the library system decided to name that facility honoring us. I am told, The Miller Branch Library on 28th Street, off Vienna Hills, is the most popular in the system. If you asked me, I think that may be due to the foresight of the leaders, in hanging a picture of Joanie in the lobby.

God continued to open doors of opportunity for me to be involved in ministry in different ways. A man named Jay Lohan came to our church to tell us about a mission need. Jay had been a farmer all his life but, like me, he sold up, and retired. Retirement didn't sit any easier with Jay than it did with me and, before long, Jay felt called to ministry. He spent many months in Equatorial Africa trying to introduce modern farming techniques in the region. By the time he walked into our church, he had moved on to Haiti, a country closer to home. He was working in Haiti to drill water wells, as the people in villages had no access to clean water.

I went to Haiti with Jay, to a little town in an area called Pignon to see for myself. When I saw what people had to endure, it just broke my heart. Some of the cities had running water, but for most of the country, the nearest river was the only source of drinking water. The same river, the Boujaja, was used for everything you can imagine. Drinking, cooking, washing clothes, watering livestock, and more. I saw cows wallowing in the same river mothers were forced to draw water from for their families. This resulted in rampant illness among the villagers, and the tiny hospital in town was overflowing with more people than it could possibly serve. There was a never-ending waiting line to get into the hospital. The few wells that did exist were very poor. The best drilling rigs they had in Haiti at that time were what we call cable tool operations. This means that a heavy metal shaft was lifted and dropped into a hole over and over again. This is one of the most primitive ways to bore a hole, and it is slow, slow, slow. One well of a few hundred feet might take an entire month to complete.

In a place like Texas, one would think nothing of drilling down 5000 feet to get water, so a couple hundred feet is an easy well to drill by comparison. When I saw what those poor people were up against, attempting to drill a water well in this primitive way, and how hard they had to work for what we would call a tiny well, I became determined to help, because it was the right thing to do. I knew what a great difference our help would make. I thank God every day for instinctively showing me what I need to do. Knowing exactly

Villagers enjoying fresh water from their well

what you need to do is a good thing. I flew back to Arkansas and put together a rotary drilling rig for Jay.

The rig we assembled was no big deal by our standards, and it would have been common on any modern water-drilling operation in America. We chartered a boat to take the rig back to Haiti. I followed to make sure things went smoothly after the rig arrived. The rig we cobbled together from spare parts could finish in a single day, what would have taken the village people twenty days, or even a month to do. We gave the finished well flowing with fresh clean water to the people of the village. It brought them hope like they had never had before.

Our rotary rig was mobile, and after we had capped one well and installed a pump jack on it, we moved to another site and did it all over again. Within a year or two we completed more than 500 new water wells. We had such great success drilling wells in Haiti that a group of people from a very large charity in Wisconsin heard about us. They began talking with us about their similar mission and I decided to leave the rotary rig we had made in Haiti for the Wisconsin group to use, which they still use to this day. This is a great example of how God multiplies all efforts, offered in His name.

In the drilling contracting business, whether the hole the crew drills is wet or dry, the driller still gets paid, but I see now that I was missing out by only getting paid. I have to say there aren't many experiences in life more satisfying than seeing a person who had only known cloudy, brown, dangerous drinking water—hauled by sheer muscle up a river bank, and then carried for miles back home —walk up to a pump, crank the handle and watch beautiful, sweet, clear water run out. I've brought in thousands of wells over my career, many of them ahead of schedule, with fat bonus payments attached, but seeing the use the Haitian people got out of those water wells, was the most satisfying thing I've put my hand to in my entire career as a drilling contractor. I felt such a profound sense of walking with the Lord when I helped drill those water wells. This was what E. Stanley Jones had been talking about when he told me God needed businessmen too. The Lord has made it possible — I didn't have to get paid. I've already been well paid. All I have needed, His hand has provided — great is your faithfulness, Lord unto me.

Bob in the woods near his home

15

NEW BEGINNINGS

My wife Joanie was a wonderful woman. I was always amazed by how deeply she felt things. I was mostly a country music fan, but could appreciate the beauty in other music, even if it wasn't the sort of thing I preferred. Joanie not only appreciated music but felt it as deeply as the people playing it. When I remember her listening to opera, the way her face would become absolutely in tune with the characters as they sung their hearts out, I remember Joanie absolutely in her element.

I have never known anyone who could live in the moment so much as Joanie. Her nephew, Kit Vinson, told me a story about driving Joanie in his new car. When he graduated from high school, his father bought him a Mustang GT convertible. This was a top of the line, speed demon model, with a 5-liter V8 and fat racing tires. Joanie and I had gone to visit Kit's parents. Kit was very proud of his new car and asked his

Aunt Joanie if she would like to see it. Joanie was delighted, and as she began to walk to the driveway where the car was parked, she started to tie a scarf over her hair. Kit asked her what she was doing. She said, "Well, you're going to take me for a ride in that thing." It was wintertime and not convertible weather, but Joanie said to Kit, "Put that top down." After they drove out onto the street Joanie told Kit to show her what the car had, and after a moment of hesitation, Kit dropped that car into second gear and peeled out. Kit said he must have left half his tires right there on the street. That was Joanie. She loved an adventure.

Toward the end of her life, Joanie suffered increasingly from bipolar disorder and epilepsy. She died one Sunday morning in January 2003. Had she lived three more months, we would have been married 53 years. It was terribly lonely after Joanie died, and for months it seemed that I would never be myself again. Our lives were together through good times and bad. We married young and had been together ever since. I felt lost without her. Then, with God's grace, after several months I realized I did not have a choice about whether or not to go on with my life. I was no different than any other person who had lost a spouse. I simply had to deal with my new reality. That realization gave me the clarity I needed. Though I would eventually go on to be with her in heaven, Joanie could never come back to me. Once I was able to acknowledge this myself, I became determined to get on with my life.

I first met Nadine Hardin through her husband, Hugh. Hugh was one of the finest lawyers in Fort Smith. I had known him for nearly thirty years. I have never been one to keep lawyers around, but Hugh had a tremendously keen mind, which I admired. Whenever I bought property like the church, which became Community Rescue Mission, I would always use Hugh's firm to make sure we got a clear title to avoid future problems.

Nadine, in her own right, is quite an accomplished woman. By her own admission, she was a white glove Southern wife and lady, who realized that no one would blame her if she chose to stay nestled in the comfort of her

Nadine Hardin Miller

home, shielded from the world and its issues. It will come as no surprise to anyone who knows Nadine, even a little, that something in her spirit rebelled against being sheltered from life. She has always enjoyed life, and she determined a long time ago that she would be a doer, not a spectator.

As wife to a busy, high-profile attorney, and Mother to four children, she always found the time to extend hospitality and care to her family and to others. Nadine was very involved in leadership roles with her church and the United Methodist Women, both statewide and globally. She has been and remains one of the pillars of our Fort Smith community. There's no telling the amount of money Nadine has raised for charitable causes, nor is there any wall big enough to display all the awards and certificates of appreciation given to her over the years. She has led such a rich and varied life, and I think the only way to do her justice, is to write another book, something I hope to do soon.

Hugh and Nadine attended the same church as Joanie and me, and our families were friends. Sadly, Hugh died in September 2000, so Nadine had already suffered the loss of her spouse and was three years ahead of me on that journey.

Nadine and I were part of the same group of friends. Occasionally our group would go out together for dinner or some type of activity, and she and I saw one another in those settings. We always enjoyed one another's company. It seemed most natural after time, that Nadine and I should marry. With Nadine, I felt the joyful, effortless passage of time, something I treasured then and now.

Nadine and I married in First United Methodist Church

in 2003. Rather than ask people to rearrange their schedules to fit a date we would choose for our ceremony, we decided to do something more practical. At the end of the regular Sunday worship service on August 17th, the pastor announced to the congregation that Nadine and I would be married immediately after the service, and all who wished to celebrate our marriage with us were invited to stay. Our friends were already lined up in their usual places in the pews! It was a sweet ceremony I will never forget, followed

Bob and Nadine Miller

by a huge luncheon-reception that hosted virtually the entire congregation. As I looked at Nadine on our wedding day, I felt like the luckiest man in the world. I have had a wonderful life, and I am thankful to have Nadine by my side.

Nadine has made my life happier than I ever thought it could be. She sees things differently than I do, and she has a keen sense about people. When I told her that I had been adopted as a baby, it was Nadine who pushed me to find out all I could about my birth parents. She took the lead and did the research with the Edna Gladney Home. Without her interest in my story, without her telling me that my story mattered and that I deserved to know, I never would have found out about my other siblings. I never would have known the life my mother led, after she gave birth to me. I went through my life up to this point, never thinking much about my biological family. Nadine changed that. When Nadine and I became our own family, I realized I had a third family, but where, I had no idea. With Nadine's tireless, dedicated help, I discovered my biological roots.

Sadly, I learned my biological Mother died nearly three-years before we started the process of our discovery. I wish I could have met my mother. It was joyous to meet a couple of my nephews, and other extended family members. Thanks to the records supplied by Edna Gladney and photo albums given to me by newly discovered family, I know more today about my biological family than I could ever expect.

Would you believe one of my stepbrothers was named Bob?

Laura May, Bob's biological mother

Bob and Nadine

16

WHAT I'D TELL MYSELF

As this story of my life is completed, I am surprised by what I see. I never much thought I had the kind of life worth writing about, so when I was asked to share my story, I didn't know how it would turn out. After all, it is a rather intimate thing to do. For many years, it just seemed like I moved from one thing to the next, but, looking back now through this wide-angle lens, I see the hand of God guiding me through the world.

The degree I was pursuing at college in husbandry, landed me the job at the college farm and taught me about ranching.

The reduced wind velocity of the typically sustained, strong Oklahoma winds, failed to produce the force needed by the windmills to pump enough water to keep the grass and livestock alive on the ranch. This unusual weather phenomena pushed us to close down the ranching operation and move back to Texas.

Because I moved back to Texas, I had to get a different job. I was no longer in ranching.

Because Joanie's father happened to have money invested in the drilling business, I got a job as a roughneck in Abilene with Mr. Gilchrist. (I suppose those reduced Oklahoma winds were still strong enough to sweep me into the drilling business in Texas.)

At Joanie's insistence, I took time to go to a Christian Ashram meeting, when I really didn't think I had the time nor money to go. (Joanie received a couple of free tickets from someone at the church we attended.)

At the Ashram meeting, I met E. Stanley Jones, whose wisdom gave me the freedom to be the best businessman I could be, with God's help, and understand I was good enough for God.

Because I got into the drilling business, I was successful enough to catch the eye of the Tulsa world, and Peter Grace, whose company bought Miller Drilling Company and, thus positioned me to retire.

In retirement I devoted myself fully to helping anyone I could with the blessings I had received.

The ways that God touches our lives aren't often visible at the moments they happen, but upon looking back they certainly are clear as day.

Truly, the three miracles I experienced when I was at my lowest point, sitting on that knoll at dawn praying my heart out for a way forward, are the underpinning for my life. It is moments like those that show you who God is and allow you to see God at work in your life. These are times when God is not mysterious, nor far away. He lets us know! I have been blessed to see three miracles happen right in front of my eyes, and even more, I was able to recognize these three miracles for what they were at the time. (Maybe that realization was my fourth miracle.)

I was blessed to meet E. Stanley Jones at the right moment in my life, just when I was seriously considering leaving the drilling business. But God worked through Brother Stanley to keep me in the drilling business, exactly where he wanted me until I could fulfill His plan. I know now God's plan was for me to help as many people as I could throughout my life. I pray I have been faithful to that plan. At least I am confident that my heart remains continually open and sensitive to God's guidance, wherever it may take me.

I hope anyone who reads this book can readily see how blessed I have been. I have had loving family, great friends, meaningful work and wonderful opportunities throughout my life. As a boy, I joined the church by my own free-will. Ever since, my inner faith has steadily grown.

Many people will say that making money or being successful is the way a person knows if he or she is living right. But God is no respecter of specific persons, and His kind mercies and blessings extend to all. Some people ask me about the secret of my success. While it's true, I have earned considerable money and been successful beyond my wildest dreams, I did not do it by myself. There is one thing you should know. When I boil it all down, I can honestly say, a faith which grows stronger and deeper over time is the only formula for a good and joyful life. I say with all certainty, that

I am fortunate and blessed by my strong belief in Jesus Christ and my personal relationship with him.

By God's grace I have come to know that we actually have two bodies, a physical and a spiritual body. Each body is equally important, and both must be fed appropriately in order to live and thrive. Physical strength requires us to eat nutritional foods. Spiritual strength comes from feeding our spiritual bodies through prayer, Bible study and by worshipping God, not just by going to church, but by walking with Jesus every day.

Sometimes we human beings make a mess of important life decisions, and much of life's misery and difficulty are the result of not knowing which choices to make. Who should I marry? What should be my major in college? What will be my ultimate career? How do I choose between job offers? Should I start a business of my own? When should I retire? In this swarm of questions and choices, I can tell you with all sincerity, there is only one question that matters: "What am I going to do about Jesus?" All of the other decisions hang on this initial one.

I have been blessed to know Jesus as intimately as I know myself, and blessed to absolutely know that He walks beside me with every step I take. This knowledge did not come to me passively or by chance. I have pursued it, and my relationship with my Creator. Because of God's grace, love, and forgiveness, I am who I am, and I am thankful.

I can imagine myself as a 20-year-old reading this book, totally astonished by it. At 20, I could have never visualized the life experiences I know today. I could have never fathomed the depth of the relationships I would have with my family and with my Lord. If I could have read this book at the age of 20, I hope I would have been just a little more confident in myself from the sheer knowledge that a Divine, unexplainable love that passes all understanding belonged to me through Christ, and it was mine for the taking.

To those 20-year olds and others who read my story, I pray you will pursue answers to the important questions in your life, and that my experiences, whatever they're worth, will inspire you to explore all that awaits you. Most of all, you can be sure God loves you, and with that love, life success is guaranteed.

You are good enough for God, and all God wants is you.

Bob at 88

"IF YOU ASK ME..."

Celebrations of Family and Friends

"Whatever we focus on determines what we become." These words of E. Stanley Jones certainly apply to the life of Bob Miller. In the brief time between writing *Tailwind*, and publishing this book, we invited a few friends and family to share their thoughts and celebrations about Bob. I regret timing did not permit us to include others who no doubt, would have loved to be a part of this project. This section of the book is included as a special surprise for Bob. I hope you enjoy what others have to say about this remarkable man.

- Jennifer Tyler

Author

Bob loves his family dearly. He loves helping others and making a difference in his community. He is generous and kind, and he is a loving man! We are fortunate at this point along the journey of our lives, to have one another in our sunset years. I am thrilled his inspiring story has now been written.

- Nadine Hardin Miller

Wife

It is hard to find adequate words to describe the admiration I have for Bob Miller. This man loves other people. A quiet man, in a world that seems to have lost its zeal for kindness, caring and humility, Bob Miller may go unnoticed. Yet to those who find themselves cast aside by society, Bob stands as a beacon of hope and safety. Bob rules over a quiet space that is filled with compassion, patience and love for those in need. He is not afraid to hear the cries of the frail or the soft voices of the weak. Bob absorbs the troubles of the poor and turns those troubles into hope and light.

- George McGill

Mayor, Fort Smith, AR

In the life of every institution, some moments define its legacy. For The Foundation for Evangelism, I can think of three: the establishment of the E. Stanley Jones Professors of Evangelism, moving the Foundation's base of operations to Lake Junaluska, N.C., and construction of a headquarters to cement its presence. Bob was there for each of these, serving as Board Chair during some of these transitional moments. Bob Miller has provided exemplary Christian-servant leadership as a trustee of The Foundation for Evangelism for 32 of the organization's nearly 70 years of ministry. He has helped us to become a catalyst to equip disciples to share the Good News of Jesus Christ.

Bob is the only remaining Lifetime Trustee of The Foundation for Evangelism, a recognition given to only three people in our history, for an exceptional level of commitment and work. Many might consider this a title of honor and an invitation to enjoy a season of recognition. Bob is NOT that person. He is a strong advocate for our ministries, and he regularly reaches out to Foundation leadership with support, encouragement, and wisdom. It is a privilege to say thank you to this wonderful disciple of Jesus Christ.

- Jane Wood

President, The Foundation for Evangelism

Ask anyone about Bob Miller and you will hear he is an inspiration! In one of my first meetings with Bob, I asked about his life and work. He told me about an amazing life-changing experience he had during the dark days of trials in the oil field. The three miracles Bob experienced were nothing short of divine intervention, and they became pivotal to his spiritual life and to his business success. Bob's business and financial success has become a triumph of many faith-based organizations, whose work and ministry furthers the Kingdom of God. His faithful generosity is an expression of Bob's love for God and people. I have heard him say on many occasions, that his success was because of God, and therefore, he needed to give back generously to the work of God. I am blessed to know Bob and Nadine Hardin Miller. The wisdom of both have enhanced my life. I want to continue to watch and learn from Bob, as I strive to be a better person and child of God.

- J. Wayne Clark

President and CEO, United Methodist Foundation of Arkansas

Among the things I admire about Dad, is his gift of relating to people from many different walks of life. Whether employees or community leaders, he is able to put them at ease so that he can communicate what is on his mind. Another admirable trait is his ability to see a need and do something about it, as he demonstrated with the founding of the Community Rescue Mission. Through this outreach to homeless people, and others, he has been able and willing to share the good news of Jesus Christ. He has lived his life with the confidence of knowing 'Whose' he is, where he has come from and where he is going. He has been an inspiration to me to live my life with the same confidence and boldness. I count it both an honor and a blessing to call him 'Dad.'

- Michael Miller

Son

Mr. Miller is a shining example of the best of humanity. He doesn't just preach his faith, he puts it into action every day. He is one of the most faithful, generous and compassionate people I've ever met. It has been a blessing and an honor to work with him.

- Tony Flippin

Oncologist and former Board Chair, Community Rescue Mission

Bob Miller's life is living proof of a biblical promise and prophesy: The more you see Jesus in others, the more others will see Jesus in you. The drumbeat of Christ's heart is "love one another," and Bob daily tunes his heart to that divine heartbeat of love. When someone asks, "Where is Jesus today?" one of my go-to responses is "Let me tell you the story of Bob Miller."

- Leonard Sweet

Best-selling author, professor, Drew University, George Fox University, Tabor College, Evangelical Seminary and founder of preachthestory.com

Bob Miller is one of the most kind and generous people I have ever known. His story tells it all. He never waivers from his commitment and promise to God. When everything came together for him in his drilling business, and throughout his life, Bob remained faithful. We could all learn a lot from Bob and his unwavering compassion!

- Dede Hutcheson

Long-time friend

I have many wonderful memories of my Dad and I treasure the positive influence he has had on my life. As a young child, he would read "The Gingham Dog and the Calico Cat" to me with mom at night, and then give me 5 kisses and 5 hugs. Unfortunately, those affectionate expressions once resulted in Dad getting the mumps. Our frequent car rides to Wichita Falls were made enjoyable and shorter by listening to Dad's stories. I am grateful for the deep love my Dad had for my Mom. His devotion to God was apparent in our home and his everlasting love for God continues to this day. Dad's compassion for those less fortunate often results in action. I

am blessed to have such a generous, kind, gentle, loving man
as my Dad.

- Marcia Clement

Daughter

The first time I met Bob and Nadine Hardin Miller was at a
seminar at Hendrix College on the influence of E. Stanley
Jones. I was aware of the generosity that the Millers had
extended to Hendrix, e.g., the Miller Center, and I was a little
intimidated and very curious about this couple who had
given so much. How little I was actually aware of their
generosity! The Bob Miller I met that day was humble,
sincere, and open—still learning and growing. In subsequent
years I became better acquainted, and in 2015, I was
privileged to become their pastor at First United Methodist
Church, Fort Smith. My knowledge of Bob now extends to
social occasions, golfing expeditions (Neither Bob nor I are
candidates for the Senior PGA tour!), and lots of church.
Through it all, I have come to know a man of unquestionable
integrity. What Bob is on the outside, he is all the way to his
core: deep faith, big heart, generous to a fault, humble in
spirit, answering a call on his life (as communicated by E.
Stanley Jones himself) to serve God as a Christian
businessman. Well done, good and faithful servant!

- The Reverend Dr. William O. (Bud) Reeves

Senior Pastor, First United Methodist Church, Fort Smith, AR

Bob Miller is a devoted servant of God. He has always been my true hero in life.

- Bennie Westphal

Long-time friend

Bob Miller exemplifies how real disciples live in real life. He loves God passionately, seeks to follow Jesus every day, leads with compassion and is generous beyond measure. Bob is deeply invested in his local church but sees his mission in the context of the entire world. For him, this is not just an aspiration, it is a reality, and that inspires me to be a more faithful Jesus-follower.

- Gary E. Muller

Resident Bishop, Arkansas Conference, The United Methodist Church

Life is full of surprises. Few compare to the joy that comes with discovering you have a special Uncle whom you have never met. Over the last few years, the May family has been blessed to meet and get to know Uncle Bob. Having lost my father to cancer twenty years ago, I am so excited to have this new relationship. My wife, Lisa, and I have stayed in their home, enjoyed family reunions, shared dinners, talked on the phone, and fallen in love with Bob and Nadine. What a precious gift from God!

- Dr. Robert K. May

Nephew

Bob is my friend and a wonderful Christian example to my family and many people in our community. Anytime, day or night, I could call on Bob and he would be there, without question. He is a kind man with our Heavenly Father in his heart. I am so blessed to know him.

- Norma Strang

Sister-in-law, Board member, Community Rescue Mission

I have known and enjoyed the close friendship of Bob Miller since I moved to Fort Smith in 1972, some 46 years ago. We met through the United Methodist Church, as Bob is, and always has been since I have known him, a devout Christian. Through those years, Bob has shown a sincere Christian concern for others by enthusiastically sharing his time and resources to help others in their time of need. Bob has a marvelous sense of humor and is always ready to hear and consider the thoughts, and sometimes contrary opinions of others. Rarely critical and always dependable, one can only be blessed by being his friend. Our families always enjoy the spirit of love that exists among us.

- C. Larry Weir

Retired engineer

It was my lucky day when I was hired to serve the Miller family as their secretary in 1985. My personal life needed the positive influence provided by Mr. Miller over the next twenty years. He has helped shape me into a more thoughtful, grateful and giving person. He has been like a father to me, extending comfort and encouragement. The experience I gained while in his employ has helped me better understand the business world I am working in today. The opportunity to get to know Mr. Miller has been a great blessing to me and my whole family.

- Linda Billingsly

Board Member, Community Rescue Mission

Bob is truly a man of God who cares for all of Gods children, especially the homeless and needy. In all of his many Christian and charitable endeavors, he seeks no glory or publicity for himself.

- Harley Strang

Brother-in-law, Board member, Community Rescue Mission

About 30 years ago, I had the responsibility of raising funds locally for basic research on heart disease, conducted in the state of Arkansas. I sent Bob Miller a letter, along with several other potential donors. Soon thereafter, Bob saw me at church and personally handed me a check for $100, which was a handsome gift at the time. In the lower left corner of the check Bob wrote: 'for Taylor Prewitt's research.' When I saw that, it dawned on me that Bob was not concerned about the details of the project. For all he knew, I might have been using test tubes in my basement at home. But he had faith in me, and he knew that if I endorsed the effort, whatever it was, that it was good enough for him. Since that time, I've worked with Bob on other major projects in the church, and particularly with Methodist Village Senior Living, where he was chairman of the board of directors when I joined in 2004. Later, when I became board chair, I continued to be inspired by Bob's example and good stewardship. I could always count on his wisdom. Bob Miller is my friend. His example of good works and philanthropy provides an outstanding model for the rest of us. He is one-of-a-kind.

- Taylor Prewitt

Retired cardiologist

When Bill and I met Bob Miller, we were impressed that he had been so brave as to marry into the group of Arkansans called the Strang Gang. We enjoy his calm way of accepting our crazy, loving, and sometime outspoken family. We admire all he has done and continues to do for our community, city and for people with less opportunities in life. We are thankful for the privilege of knowing him.

- Freda and Bill Strang

Sister-in-law and Brother-in-law

We have known Bob Miller for many years, even before he became a member of our extended family by marrying Nadine. Our family knew of Bob's reputation as a successful oil and gas driller. We admired how he used his success to start and support several important ministries in Fort Smith, especially the Community Rescue Mission and the Antioch for

Youth and Family organization. Bob and Nadine have now been married for several years, and both share a mutual concern for people. Bob has often said that his fortune was God's money. He has avidly fulfilled his Christian devotion.

- Ernestine and Thomas Cuthbert

Sister-in-law and Brother-in-law

Bob Miller and I grew up together and enjoyed many good times as teenagers, like riding our horses along the Wichita River. Our friendship has grown over the years. We were both in the oil business. Bob had a drilling company in Abilene, Texas and my company was in Fort Smith, Arkansas. I asked him if he would have an interest in moving his rigs to Fort Smith, where I was drilling wells at that time. He accepted my invitation and I was happy to have him nearby. I think Bob may credit me with his move to Arkansas. After long successful careers, both Bob and I sold our companies. Though no longer in the drilling business, we remain friends to this day. Bob is truly a good man whom I admire. He continues to use his resources to help others in need.

- Steve Gose

Longtime friend and business associate

Bob Miller's own vocational journey, inspired by the teachings of evangelist E. Stanley Jones, and his own faith journey as a United Methodist, models the kind of reflection and action we desire for students at Hendrix College.

Through his incredible work ethic and generosity, Mr. Miller's contribution to Hendrix ensures that generations will be undergirded by their faith, as they act for the common good. Both Bob and Nadine Miller's legacy will live on in the Miller Center for Vocation, Ethics, and Calling at Hendrix College where we invite students to engage in civic and religious volunteerism around the world. We are deeply grateful for Bob's continued vision.

- The Reverend J. J. Whitney

Chaplain, Hendrix College

Bob Miller is a spiritual force, fueled by his love for God. The first time I heard him pray, it felt like God was sitting beside him and listening to what was on Bob's mind. It was truly evident to me that God and Bob Miller were old friends.

- Debbie Krause

Board member, Community Rescue Mission

A Few of Bob's Favorite Reads

From the E. Stanley Jones Foundation

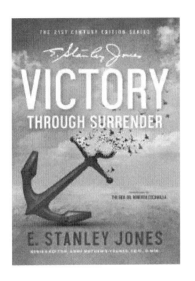

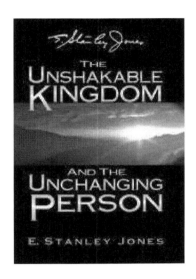

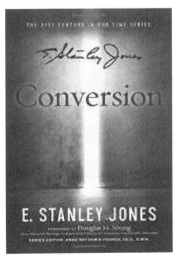

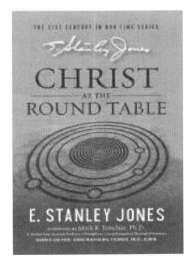

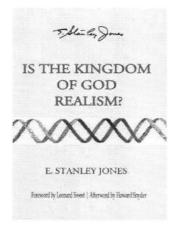

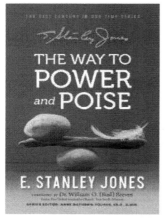

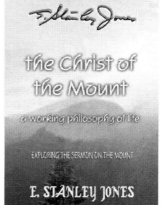

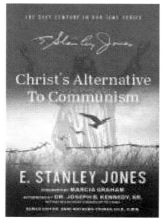

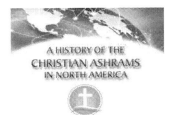

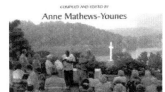

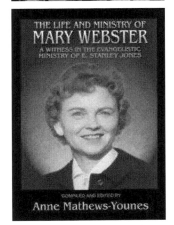

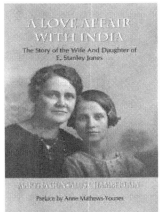

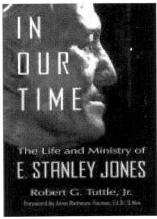

E. STANLEY JONES BOOKS

HERITAGE OF FAITH
FOR TODAY'S GENERATION

2025 will be the 100th year that the Methodist Publishing House (Abingdon Press) has kept at least one book in print by E. Stanley Jones. The E. Stanley Jones Foundation will commemorate this 100-year benchmark in partnership with Abingdon Press.

ALL PUBLICATIONS OF

The E. Stanley Jones Foundation
are available for purchase from:

www.estanleyjonesfoundation.com
and
www.amazon.com

Order your copies today!

Welcomes your support

Our Mission

The E. Stanley Jones Foundation (ESJF) exists to reach today's generations with the life-transforming message of Jesus Christ, and to equip effective Christian evangelism by making available to all, the relevant and rich works of Dr. E. Stanley Jones, whose Christ-centered preaching, teaching, and prolific writings continue to enlighten and bless millions of people worldwide.

Our Vision

- To ensure that E. Stanley Jones resources are available to the public from trusted retailers and online providers, as well as directly from the E. Stanley Jones Foundation.

- Fully equip disciples of Jesus Christ for effective evangelism.

- Use all available technological and media platforms to update, create, and distribute worldwide, the full array of Dr. Jones' books, sermons, and teaching tools to entities, including but not limited to universities, seminaries, churches, groups, and individuals.

- Create new opportunities for teaching and equipping leaders, using our timely, effective teaching tools, curricula, and training resources.

- Develop partnerships and nurture relationships with others of like mind to help ensure resources are available to implement and perpetuate our mission.

Friends Partner with us

to Fulfill our Mission

The E. Stanley Jones Foundation is a nonprofit 501(c)(3) organization. The US Internal Revenue Service Code permits the amount that US residents donate which exceeds the fair market value of the material(s) a donor receives from the Foundation to be tax-deductible. Proceeds from the sale of books and materials remain in the Foundation to continue the work of the Foundation. For more information please visit our website:

www.estanleyjonesfoundation.com

Follow us on social media

The E. Stanley Jones Foundation
10804 Fox Hunt Lane
Potomac, Maryland 20854
Phone: 240.328.5115

About the Authors

JENNIFER TYLER is the President of Tyler Associates, a national consulting firm specializing in development and fundraising for faith-based non-profits. She has a B.A. in Sociology from Louisiana College, Pineville, LA, and lives in Denton, TX.

NICHOLAS YOUNES is a graduate of St. John's College, Annapolis, MD, and has an M.F.A. in Fiction and Non-Fiction Writing from Johns Hopkins University. He lives in North Bethesda, Maryland.

Made in the USA
Columbia, SC
01 July 2019